T0368818

THE Art & SCIENCE OF TEACHING PRIMARY READING

CHRISTOPHER SUCH

CORWIN

SAGE Publications Ltd
1 Oliver's Yard
55 City Road
London EC1Y 1SP

CORWIN
A SAGE company
2455 Teller Road
Thousand Oaks, California 91320
(800) 233-9936
www.corwin.com

SAGE Publications India Pvt Ltd
B 1/I 1 Mohan Cooperative Industrial Area
Mathura Road
New Delhi 110 044

SAGE Publications Asia-Pacific Pte Ltd
3 Church Street
#10-04 Samsung Hub
Singapore 049483

© Christopher Such 2021

Editor: James Clark
Assistant editor: Diana Alves
Production editor: Martin Fox
Marketing manager: Dilhara Attygalle
Cover design: Wendy Scott
Typeset by: C&M Digitals (P) Ltd, Chennai, India
Printed in the UK

Library of Congress Control Number: 2020951170

British Library Cataloguing in Publication data

A catalogue record for this book is available from the British Library

ISBN 978-1-5297-6417-8
ISBN 978-1-5297-6416-1 (pbk)

At SAGE we take sustainability seriously. Most of our products are printed in the UK using responsibly sourced papers and boards. When we print overseas we ensure sustainable papers are used as measured by the PREPS grading system. We undertake an annual audit to monitor our sustainability.

This book is dedicated to the memory of Andrew Currie.

CONTENTS

ABOUT THE AUTHOR

Christopher Such is a primary school teacher from Peterborough, England. He has worked in education for over fourteen years, teaching reading to children in every year group from reception to Year 6. Since 2019 he has contributed to the initial teacher training programme at Teach East, delivering courses on evidence-informed reading instruction and mathematics. He is currently a senior leader at Fulbridge Academy responsible for curriculum improvement and professional development. He is also the author of the education blog, Primary Colour, and can be found on Twitter via the username @Suchmo83.

ACKNOWLEDGEMENTS

First, I would like to thank SAGE Publishing, who saw value in what I had written and helped me to make the book into something of greater value.

Second, I would like to thank all the colleagues that have generously nudged me in the right direction through my teaching career, especially Jules Perry, Emma Green, Heidi Philby, Laura Hurrell, Hollie Stafford, Katie Wilson and Andrew Currie.

Third, I would like to thank Neil Almond, Lloyd Williams-Jones, Kieran Mackle, Elliot Morgan, Shannen Doherty and Matt Swain. Their support and encouragement provided the initial impetus for this book, and their feedback once it was written was invaluable.

Finally, I would like to thank my family, in particular my wonderful mum, Jennifer Such, and my wife, Silvia Janurova, who I love more than I am able to express in words.

INTRODUCTION

Few impediments undermine a person's aspirations as effectively as an inability to read. Around one in six people in England are functionally illiterate, meaning that they have difficulty reading about unfamiliar topics or from unfamiliar sources.[1] Such basic reading difficulties are correlated with many of society's most challenging ills. Illiteracy turns everyday life into a struggle, disempowering and alienating people from their own society. It also deprives people of the joy and fulfilment that the written word has to offer. Thus, teaching children to read is one of the most important duties of every school, one that necessitates a foundation of knowledge upon which classroom practice can be based. Teachers must know what reading entails, how children learn to do it and, consequently, how it can be taught most effectively.

Teaching reading is an art that relies on instincts honed by experience, so the attempt to rationalise it through the lens of scientific research can seem reductive and ill-conceived. However, this is not the case. The art of teaching can, and should, be informed and strengthened by an understanding of the science of reading. This book is my attempt to demonstrate this and to fast-track educators through a process that has taken me more than a decade.

Despite decades of research into the subject, studies from across several countries reinforce what my experience has suggested, namely that many teachers are inexcusably ill-informed about reading.[2] To some, this is an indication of the malignant effects of the 'reading wars', in which evidence-informed approaches to reading instruction, particularly the systematic teaching of phonics, have for generations been pitted against contrasting ineffective methods. However, there are also more banal reasons why many educators have insufficient knowledge on the subject of reading research: teachers are time-poor, often working long hours in stressful environments.[3] In addition, too few schools prioritise professional reading; it is not uncommon to meet teachers, including reading coordinators, who have undertaken no professional reading since their initial teacher training, with their schools having done nothing to ameliorate this. Perhaps most importantly, much of what has been written on the subject of reading instruction has not been tailored to the needs of primary teachers. With all this in mind, the aim of this book is to provide educators with a brief yet essential guide to the science behind reading and its practical implications for the art of classroom teaching. I hope you find it to be valuable.

A brief overview

This book is divided into six parts:

Part I provides a whirlwind tour of the history of reading and writing before explaining the factors that make learning to read in English so difficult. It concludes by introducing a framework through which reading can be approached and understood.

Part II describes the process of decoding and how it can be taught, considering phonics in all its forms and the development of reading fluency.

Part III analyses exactly what goes on in the mind of someone who is deriving meaning as they read. It then discusses the intertwining components that make up expert reading comprehension and how these can be fostered in the classroom.

Part IV considers other opportunities for reading across the school curriculum, including disciplinary reading, writing and independent reading.

Part V explains how to address reading difficulties through a discussion of dyslexia, assessment and intervention.

Each chapter of the first five parts follows a similar structure in which the body of the chapter is followed by a brief summary, a discussion of other classroom implications, questions for further professional discussions, a retrieval quiz and suggestions for further reading.

Part VI synthesises the evidence from Parts I to V, describing how a balanced reading diet can be created to improve outcomes for all children. It concludes with action plans for classroom teachers and reading coordinators.

Which reading science should we prioritise?

The aim of this book is to detail the science related to reading instruction and to consider how this can be intertwined with the art of classroom teaching. Nevertheless, the interpretation of reading science is hotly contested. Despite there existing something close to consensus among reading experts on most of the key aspects of reading described in this book, differences in opinion remain, of course. Much of these appear to come about due to individuals' levels of caution in interpreting different forms of research.[4] Some are intrigued by the possibilities of research into cognitive science, but strongly prioritise research studies conducted in actual classrooms, known as applied research; others are a little bolder in extrapolating from the findings of cognitive science. I admit to leaning towards the former position. Teaching is a wonderfully complicated business, and I'm much more convinced by methods that have been shown to work in the whirling complexity of real classrooms than by studies that suggest that something *should* work based on what we have learned in other contexts. Nevertheless, the applied research of classroom studies currently leaves us with some gaps in our understanding of what is most likely to be effective. In these cases, it is most sensible to combine the hints gained from cognitive science with knowledge from years of teaching to derive recommendations for classroom practice. The resulting recommendations are our best bets for improving reading outcomes for all children.

References

1   National Literacy Trust (n.d.). *Information on Adult Literacy in the UK*. Available at: https://literacytrust.org.uk/parents-and-families/adult-literacy/ (accessed 30 November 2020).
2   Aro, M. and Björn, P. M. (2016). Preservice and inservice teachers' knowledge of language constructs in Finland. *Annals of Dyslexia*, 66, 111–126; Fielding-Barnsley, R. (2010). Australian pre-service teachers' knowledge of phonemic awareness and phonics in the process of learning to read. *Australian Journal of Learning Difficulties*, 15, 99–110; Hurry, J., Nunes, T., Bryant, P., Pretzlik, U., Parker, M., Curno, T. and Midgley, L. (2005). Transforming research on morphology into teacher practice. *Research Papers in Education*, 20, 187–206; Moats, L. (2009). Still wanted: Teachers with knowledge of language. *Journal of Learning Disabilities*, 42, 387–391.
3   Sellgren, K. (2019). Teachers 'have worked long hours for many years'. BBC News, 18 September. Available at: www.bbc.com/news/education-49728831 (accessed 6 January 2021).
4   Shanahan, T. (2020). What constitutes a science of reading instruction? *Reading Research Quarterly*, 55(S1), S235–S437.

Part I

Reading and its Origins

1

A BRIEF HISTORY OF READING AND WRITING

Spoken language is arguably humanity's greatest invention. It allows us to share our thoughts with anyone, assuming they possess a shared grasp of the words being used and of the grammar organising them into meaningful ideas. To understand how we read – and to avoid the misconceptions that frequently plague the teaching of reading – we must first comprehend the nature of writing and how this relates to spoken language. To achieve this, a brief detour into the history and purposes of the written word is necessary.

Despite their superficial differences, all modern written languages share one fundamental similarity: they all represent the sounds of spoken language.[1] Writing did not begin this way, however. Humans have been creating images to represent objects in the real world for over 30,000 years, the rough age of the earliest cave paintings.[2] (Some scholars also believe that these representational images signify a watershed in human imagination and the inception of all art and science.)[3] These pictures that directly represented objects, called pictographs, were the first attempt to communicate across time, beyond the limits of spoken sounds, and are thus the beginnings of all writing. The crucial step that followed, one that took tens of thousands of years to achieve, was for these pictures to begin to represent the spoken words related to the objects, rather than the objects themselves. (Once a symbol – whether it is pictographic or not – begins to represent a word, it is called a logograph.) This was a leap of imagination, severing the link between images and the things they represent. It set the stage for the next essential development, one that relied on uniquely human capacities of association: symbolic representations of words that were not pictographic, i.e. symbols that did not depict a word directly in pictures.[4] These non-pictographic logographs made it possible, in theory at least, to represent the entirety of a spoken language and with it every thought and idea that could be expressed in words. In practice, however, there was a snag: evidence taken from the study of early written languages suggests an upper limit to the number of individual symbols that humans can memorise in a functional written language, around 2000–5000.[5] Given that the average English speaker has a vocabulary that far exceeds this limit (something also true for the vast majority of languages), a purely logographic written language simply can't represent the entire spoken language.[6] The final step, one that is evident in every modern written language, solved this problem by representing the *individual sounds* that constitute words. In this way, entire spoken languages can be represented by a relatively small number of symbols, few enough to allow for effective memorisation.

This raises two important questions: what sounds are represented within a given written language and why are these units of sound chosen? Written English functions by representing the smallest recognisable units of spoken sound, **phonemes**, via an alphabet. However, many languages are written by representing larger units of sound. Written Japanese, for example, uses individual symbols to represent entire syllables (alongside logographic symbols called *kanji*). Why is this? All spoken languages could theoretically be written using an alphabet representing the various phonemes of a language, so why do so many written languages represent larger units of sound? In a word, efficiency. While some academics have inaccurately suggested that alphabetic written languages are more 'evolved' than others, this isn't the case.[7] Written languages represent the units of sound that most efficiently match the spoken language. The spoken syllables of Japanese can be represented by around 100 symbols. (Collectively, these symbols are known as a syllabary.) Hebrew is more efficiently written and read when only the consonants are represented.[8] In comparison, spoken English, like most Indo-European languages, contains far too many different syllables (around 15,000, though estimates vary) to be written with a syllabary, and it lacks the underlying structure to be written with just consonants.[9] Written English represents individual phonemes, not because this is somehow better than representing larger units of sound, but because there is no other way to represent spoken English.[10] The sound unit used in a writing system must match the spoken language.[11] In English, this sound unit is the phoneme, and the letter or group of letters used to represent a phoneme is called a **grapheme**. The idea that there is a systematic relationship between graphemes and phonemes in languages written with an alphabet is called the **alphabetic principle**.

What is the purpose of knowing all this? Why must we know that written English – and thus the reading of English – is built around the smallest units of sound, called phonemes? First, we must grasp that reading and writing are two sides of the same coin, that the writing of English is the encoding of units of sound onto a page using an alphabet and that the reading of English is the decoding of those symbols to retrieve the sounds. Second, we must know that phonemes are the units of sound upon which English writing and reading are built. Teachers who grasp these two principles are much more likely to teach reading in a way that aligns with the fundamental logic of written English, increasing their students' chances of success.

——————————————— In a nutshell … ———————————————

- All modern written languages represent units of sound; the sound unit chosen matches the structure of the spoken language.
- In English, the sound units represented are the smallest distinct sound units, called phonemes.

Other implications for the classroom

There is a key idea contained within this chapter that will be a recurring theme through the book: understanding the underlying principles of a concept provides a stable foundation for practical classroom choices. It is one thing to be *told* why something works; it is another thing entirely to *understand* why something works. The former is liable to 'lethal mutations', where sensible ideas morph over time into something of little use; the latter is a much more robust basis for teaching.[12]

——————————— Questions for professional discussions ———————————

- Given the history of reading and writing described in this chapter, at what point do children's first attempts at mark making truly become writing in any form? When do they become writing in English?
- How might the teaching of reading (and writing) differ in languages where a syllabary can be used to represent the syllables of the language?

——————————————— Retrieval quiz ———————————————

1   What is a pictograph?
2   What is a logograph?
3   What is a phoneme?
4   What is a grapheme?
5   Why would it be impossible for a person to learn to read in English by simply memorising words as whole units?

Further reading

- Seidenberg, M. (2017). *Language at the Speed of Sight: How We Read, Why So Many Can't, and What Can Be Done About It*. New York: Basic Books.

- Willingham, D. T. (2017). *The Reading Mind: A Cognitive Approach to Understanding How the Mind Reads*. Hoboken, NJ: John Wiley & Sons.
- Wolf, M. (2008). *Proust and the Squid: The Story and Science of the Reading Brain*. New York: Harper Perennial.

References

1   McGuinness, D. (2006). *Early Reading Instruction: What Science Really Tells Us About How to Teach Reading*. Cambridge, MA: MIT Press.
2   Seidenberg, M. (2017). *Language at the Speed of Sight: How We Read, Why So Many Can't, and What Can Be Done About It*. New York: Basic Books.
3   Bronowski, J. (2011). *The Ascent of Man*. London: BBC Books.
4   Wolf, M. (2008). *Proust and the Squid: The Story and Science of the Reading Brain*. New York: Harper Perennial.
5   Mair, V. H. (1996). Modern Chinese writing. In Daniels, P. T. and Bright, W. (eds), *The World's Writing Systems*, New York: Oxford University Press, 200–208; Akamatsu, N. (2006). Literacy acquisition in Japanese–English bilinguals. In Joshi, R. M. and Aaron, P. G. (eds), *Handbook of Orthography and Literacy*. Mahwah, NJ: Lawrence Erlbaum Associates, 481–496.
6   Brysbaert, M., Stevens, M., Mandera, P. and Keuleers, E. (2016). How many words do we know? Practical estimates of vocabulary size dependent on word definition, the degree of language input and the participant's age. *Frontiers in Psychology*, 7, 1116.
7   Gelb, I. J. (1963). *A Study of Writing*. Chicago, IL: University of Chicago Press; McGuinness, *Early Reading Instruction*.
8   Seidenberg (2017).
9   McGuinness (2006).
10 Ibid.
11 Castles, A., Rastle, K. and Nation, K. (2018). Ending the reading wars: Reading acquisition from novice to expert. *Psychological Science in the Public Interest*, 19(1), 5–51.
12 Schauble, L. and Glaser, R. (eds) (2013). *Innovations in Learning: New Environments for Education*. London: Routledge.

2

USEFUL FRAMEWORKS FOR READING COMPREHENSION

Due to its importance, the nature of how humans learn to read is one of the most studied aspects of human cognition.[1] In an attempt to understand the necessary components of skilled reading, Gough and Tunmer (1986) proposed a '**simple view of reading**' in which reading comprehension was seen as a function of merely two components: decoding – the ability to work out the sounds represented by written words – and language comprehension – the ability to interpret what the words mean individually and together.[2] Given that skilled reading was considered to be impossible if either component was entirely lacking, it was expressed as the following equation:

Decoding (D) × Language Comprehension (LC) = Reading Comprehension (RC)

The simple view of reading is supported by the fact that it is possible for a person's reading comprehension to falter despite good decoding if their language comprehension is weak, and vice versa. In addition, there is evidence that different underlying skills predict word reading and language comprehension through primary school and have been shown to be differentially important for reading comprehension as children age. Decoding and language comprehension explain almost all of the variation between people's ability to read.[3] The simple view is, in short, a useful way to think about reading, especially due to the way in which it makes clear the need for fluent decoding.[4] Nevertheless, the simple view of reading does not tell us how to teach.[5] It would be easy to assume from this framework that the teaching of reading requires only instruction in decoding and then development of one's understanding of spoken language. This would be an error.[6] There is evidence that people's listening comprehension and reading comprehension are correlated, but not perfectly so, and the extent of this correlation varies with age.[7] Oral language and written language also differ in both their complexity – the latter being more complex – and in the extent to which they use words that anchor the audience in the present context.[8] In short, the utility of the simple view of reading depends on understanding that both of its components – decoding and language comprehension – are multivariate and require analysis.

Reading comprehension defined

Snow (2002) defined reading comprehension as, 'the process of simultaneously extracting and constructing meaning through interaction and involvement with written language' (p. 11).[9] Similarly, Castles, Rastle and Nation (2018) defined reading comprehension as, 'the orchestrated product of a set of linguistic and cognitive processes operating on text and interacting with background knowledge, features of the text, and the purpose and goals of the reading situation' (p. 28).[10] Although brief definitions may be of use to some, in practical terms reading comprehension is best considered as the construction of meaning from text by integrating all of the elements that will be discussed in the remainder of this book.

──────────────── In a nutshell … ────────────────

- Reading can be considered to be the product of decoding and language comprehension, where weaknesses in either will lead to difficulties with reading comprehension.

Other implications for the classroom

It is tempting sometimes to look at the results of reading comprehension tests and attempt to work backwards to the difficulties that children may be having. The simple view of reading shows that this is not likely to be successful. First, reading comprehension difficulties can occur even when a child has excellent language comprehension if they struggle to decode, and vice versa. Second, as will be discussed in the coming chapters, decoding and language comprehension are both multivariate entities whose components need to be understood in isolation if we are to identify and ameliorate children's difficulties with reading comprehension.

──────────── Questions for professional discussions ────────────

- Britton (1970) described reading (and writing) as 'floating on a sea of talk'.[11] To what extent is this idea represented by the simple view of reading? What, if anything, is missing?
- What are the potential advantages and disadvantages of teachers sharing a relatively simple definition of reading comprehension, such as that contained within a single sentence or equation?

──────────── Retrieval quiz ────────────

1 What entities are represented in the equation of the simple view of reading?
2 Why would it be an error to interpret the simple view of reading as showing that teachers need only concern themselves with children's ability to decode and their oral language abilities?

Further reading

- Castles, A., Rastle, K. and Nation, K. (2018). Ending the reading wars: Reading acquisition from novice to expert. *Psychological Science in the Public Interest*, 19(1), 5–51.
- Hoover, W. A. and Gough, P. B. (1990). The simple view of reading. *Reading and Writing*, 2(2), 127–160.

References

1 Rayner, K., Foorman, B. R., Perfetti, C. A., Pesetsky, D. and Seidenberg, M. S. (2001). How psychological science informs the teaching of reading. *Psychological Science in the Public Interest*, 2(2), 31–74.
2 Gough, P. B. and Tunmer, W. E. (1986). Decoding, reading, and reading disability. *Remedial and Special Education*, 7(1), 6–10; Hoover, W. A. and Gough, P. B. (1990). The simple view of reading. *Reading and Writing*, 2(2), 127–160.
3 Lervåg, A., Hulme, C. and Melby-Lervåg, M. (2018). Unpicking the developmental relationship between oral language skills and reading comprehension: It's simple, but complex. *Child Development*, 89(5), 1821–1838.
4 Rose, J. (2006). *Independent Review of the Teaching of Early Reading – Final Report.* Available at: https://webarchive.nationalarchives.gov.uk/20100512233640/http:// publications.teachernet.gov.uk/eOrderingDownload/0201-2006PDF-EN-01.pdf (accessed 7 January 2021).

5   Castles, A., Rastle, K. and Nation, K. (2018). Ending the reading wars: Reading acquisition from novice to expert. *Psychological Science in the Public Interest*, 19(1), 5–51.

6   Shanahan, T. (2020). *Why Following the Simple View May Not Be Such a Good Idea.* Shanahan on Literacy, 7 March. Available at: https://shanahanonliteracy.com/blog/why-following-the-simple-view-may-not-be-such-a-good-idea (accessed 7 January 2021).

7   Megherbi, H. and Ehrlich, M. F. (2004). Oral comprehension in young children who are good and bad at understanding written texts. *The Psychological Year*, 104(3), 433–489; Shanahan, T. and Lonigan, C. J. (2010). The National Early Literacy Panel: A summary of the process and the report. *Educational Researcher*, 39(4), 279–285; Catts, H. W., Hogan, T. P. and Adolf, S. M. (2005). Developmental changes in reading and reading disabilities. In Catts, H. W. and Kamhi, A. G. (eds), *The Connections Between Language and Reading Disabilities*. New York: Psychology Press, 25–40.

8   Montag, J. L., Jones, M. N. and Smith, L. B. (2015). The words children hear: Picture books and the statistics for language learning. *Psychological Science*, 26(9), 1489–1496; Oakhill, J., Cain, K. and Elbro, C. (2014). *Understanding and Teaching Reading Comprehension: A Handbook*. London: Routledge.

9   Snow, C. (2002). *Reading for understanding: Toward an R&D program in reading comprehension*. Santa Monica, CA: Rand Corporation, 11.

10 Castles, Rastle and Nation (2018), 28.

11 Britton, J. (1970). *Language and Learning*. New York: Penguin Books, 7.

3

THE TROUBLE WITH ENGLISH

If reading entails the decoding of spellings to access the encoded sounds and then interpreting the meaning of these sounds, why is it such a difficult skill to learn? And how can we teach it well? To begin to answer these questions, we must consider what decoding written English entails. For the purposes of this discussion, it is necessary to point out a typographical convention of this book: sounds will be represented using letters inside a pair of forward slashes (e.g. /ch/), and spellings will be represented using letters inside angle brackets (e.g. <ch>).

As McGuinness (2006) states, 'All codes are reversible mapping systems' (p. 12).[1] This means that a writer needs to **encode** the words they can hear in their mind into the spellings that represent their constituent sounds; conversely, the reader needs to **decode** the sounds from the spellings. Put simply, the writer turns sounds into written letters; the reader does the reverse. The trouble is that the phonemes – the units of sound being represented in written English – can be represented in multiple ways (e.g. the /ch/ phoneme can be represented by both <ch> and <tch> graphemes). Equally, the graphemes – the letters or groups of letters used to represent individual phonemes – can represent multiple sounds, the identity of each depending on the specific word they are in (e.g. the grapheme <or> represents different sounds in the words 'fork' and 'work'.). Not all languages are quite so opaque. In fact, English is almost uniquely difficult to decode. The extent to which the graphemes and phonemes deviate from a simple one-to-one correspondence is called **orthographic depth**, and English has an exceptionally deep **orthography**.[2] (Orthography merely means the conventional spelling system of a language.) This has come about due to the long and complicated history of written English, including the adoption and assimilation of words from various languages and changes in common pronunciation not reflected in English orthography.[3] Languages with relatively deep orthographies are more challenging to decode, and learning to do so takes significantly more time for the average student.[4] It is undeniably tricky to teach the code through which the writing and reading of English is conducted.

It is easy, however, to overstate the unpredictability of English orthography. A common refrain of those with limited understanding of the subject is that written English is just too complicated to fit any set of rules and consequently that any attempt to teach children to decode systematically is ill-judged. The initial premise is partly correct, but the conclusion is patently false. While English does indeed have a deep orthography that undermines any attempt to impart simple *rules* relating to its spelling, it is also not random or entirely unpredictable.[5] Teachers need to understand the connections between the approximately 44 phonemes in spoken English (depending on accent) and the various graphemes that represent them so that they can teach these connections to children in a way that makes most sense.[6] This is the aim of systematic phonics instruction, the focus of the next chapter.

─────────────── In a nutshell … ───────────────

- Understand that written English, like all written languages, is a *code* representing the sounds of spoken English.
- Know that the units of sound upon which English writing is built are phonemes, the smallest units of sound; thus, the teaching of early reading should revolve around the teaching of these units of sound, rather than larger units such as syllables.
- Understand that English orthography, despite its complexity, is something that can be systematically related to the sounds represented by spellings.

Other implications for the classroom

The deep orthography of English has confounded classroom teachers for generations. It is essential to grasp the ways in which the complexities of the code make learning to read more difficult for children and to act accordingly. In practice, this means ensuring that children come to appreciate that the code of English does not have simple, consistent correspondences between letters and sounds, and that the relationships between them depends on the individual word. This can be a delicate balancing act. Children are likely to be overwhelmed if they are immediately introduced to the full complexity of these correspondences in English orthography. Equally, hiding this complexity entirely may lead to children being confused when new sound–spelling correspondences are introduced. Gradually exposing children to the challenging orthography of English requires the use of a structured systematic phonics programme, something that will be discussed in the next chapter. It also requires careful judgement in the classroom to ensure children are exposed to the intricacies of English in a way that matches their development and confidence. Just as students of science may be introduced to necessarily simplified models of phenomena (e.g. the planetary model of the atom) that are stepping stones to an increasingly nuanced understanding, so too should children's grasp of the complexities of English orthography be carefully managed over time. Nevertheless, from almost the very beginning of their journey of learning to read, children should be introduced to the fundamental idea that individual sounds can be represented by multiple spellings and that individual spellings can represent multiple sounds.

──────── Questions for professional discussions ────────

- In what ways might teaching children to decode be different if English had a shallow orthography? Why?
- The Estonian language has an exceptionally shallow orthography. If a child arrived to your class who had learned to read Estonian, but had not encountered English writing before, what challenges might this child face? How might you support the child in their first steps of learning to read English?

──────── Retrieval quiz ────────

1   What is meant by orthography?
2   What is the difference between a deep orthography and a shallow orthography?
3   Diane McGuinness described all codes as 'reversible mapping systems'. What does this mean in the context of reading and writing?

Further reading

- McGuinness, D. (2006). *Early Reading Instruction: What Science Really Tells Us About How to Teach Reading*. Cambridge, MA: MIT Press.
- Seidenberg, M. (2017). *Language at the Speed of Sight: How We Read, Why So Many Can't, and What Can Be Done About It*. New York: Basic Books.

References

1   McGuinness, D. (2006). *Early Reading Instruction: What Science Really Tells Us About How to Teach Reading*. Cambridge, MA: MIT Press, 12.

2   Frost, R. and Katz, M. (eds) (1992). *Orthography, Phonology, Morphology and Meaning*. Amsterdam: Elsevier; Viise, N. M., Richards, H. C. and Pandis, M. (2011). Orthographic depth and spelling acquisition in Estonian and English: a comparison of two diverse alphabetic languages. *Scandinavian Journal of Educational Research*, 55(4), 425–453.

3   *Why English Is Just So Darned Difficult to Decode – A Short History*. The Reading Ape. Available at: www.thereadingape.com/single-post/2018/03/30/Why-English-is-just-so-darned-difficult-to-decode-a-short-history (accessed 30 November 2020).

4   Ellis, N. C. and Hooper, A. M. (2001). Why learning to read is easier in Welsh than in English: Orthographic transparency effects evinced with frequency-matched tests. *Applied Psycholinguistics*, 22(4), 571–599; Seidenberg, M. (2017). *Language at the Speed of Sight: How We Read, Why So Many Can't, and What Can Be Done About It*. New York: Basic Books.

5   Castles, A., Rastle, K. and Nation, K. (2018). Ending the reading wars: Reading acquisition from novice to expert. *Psychological Science in the Public Interest*, 19(1), 5–51; Moats, L. C. (2005). How spelling supports reading. *American Educator*, 6(12–22), 42.

6   Kroese, J. M., Mather, N. and Sammons, J. (2006). The relationship between nonword spelling abilities of K-3 teachers and student spelling outcomes. *Learning Disabilities: A Multidisciplinary Journal*, 14(2), 85–89; *Sounds-Write English Spellings: A Lexicon*. Sounds-Write. Available at: https://www.sounds-write.co.uk/sites/soundswrite/uploads/files/49-sounds_write_english_spellings_lexicon.pdf (accessed 30 November 2020).

Part II

Decoding

4

PHONICS

What is phonics?

Phonics is the teaching of within-word correspondences between the phonemes of spoken English and the graphemes of written English, referred to hereafter as **sound–spelling correspondences**. Once the nature of our writing system is understood, the importance of phonics instruction becomes obvious. Too many teachers are ill-equipped to teach phonics precisely because they have not grasped the essential idea that writing represents sounds and that in English the sounds represented are phonemes.[1]

I have lost count of the number of teachers I have spoken to who have asked some version of the following question: 'I wasn't taught phonics, so how did I learn to read?' There is no way to answer this precisely without knowing the history of the person asking the question. Some may have been taught the links between sounds and spellings by their teachers or parents/carers, so will have learned at least some phonics, though perhaps in an unsystematic way. Others may have been part of the lucky few able to derive the sound–spelling correspondences of English from mere exposure to print (just as some may learn to swim merely by being thrown in the deep end of a swimming pool). However, there can be no doubt; every person who becomes a fluent reader in English *has* grasped the links between the phonemes of spoken English and the graphemes that represent them, regardless of whether they were explicitly shown these links or whether they deduced them for themselves.

How can I be so confident in saying that every fluent reader has grasped the connections between graphemes and phonemes? Surely, there are other ways of becoming a fluent reader? Quite simply, the answer is no, there are not. There are, in effect, only two *theoretical* alternatives to learning to link the letters on a page to the sounds they represent: (a) memorising entire words, or (b) working out words based on contextual guesswork and picture cues. Let's address each of these in turn.

As discussed in Chapter 1, there appears to be an upper limit to the number of distinct symbols that can be learned and associated with given words, estimated at around 2,000–2,500 stored in long-term memory, according to McGuinness (2006).[2] As an actual reading strategy, the guessing of whole-words is predictive of subsequent reading failure.[3] (I have encountered several high-attaining, verbally skilled children whose reading progress has come to a shuddering halt at the age of 7–10 years because their reading has depended on decoding the first couple of letters a word and then guessing the rest; this strategy falls apart as the children in question meet more complicated texts.) We do not learn words as whole units.[4] Learning to read this way is a dead end.

Reading words based on contextual guesswork and picture cues – often called **cueing systems** – is an equally ineffective way to learn to read, and there is abundant evidence that such reading strategies are the preserve of poor readers.[5] Nonetheless, advocation of such strategies for early readers is still disappointingly common in schools.

Crucially, there is evidence to strongly suggest that most poor readers are limited by their poor sound–letter (i.e. phonics) skills, and thus that fluent reading relies on decoding.[6] Furthermore, the evidence base for the teaching of phonics is well-established.[7] In particular, there is strong evidence that the teaching of phonics in an explicit, systematic fashion – one which clearly introduces and then revises the most common sound–spelling correspondences in a logical order, starting with the most common – is beneficial for all students and essential for many.[8]

Types of phonics

The label of 'systematic phonics' hides a great deal of variety in the methods used to teach sound–spelling correspondences and their interaction within words. Parker (2018) divides the teaching of phonics into two categories: 'top-down' phonics and 'bottom-up' phonics.[9] Let's explore these two approaches to phonics in a little more detail.

Top-down phonics

In top-down approaches, the teaching of sound–spelling correspondences begins with whole words, and progresses from there down to the individual relationships between graphemes and phonemes. This relies upon children memorising a sizeable cache of sight words from which the correspondences can then be derived. Within this category of top-down approaches, there are two variations: **analytic phonics** and **analogy phonics**. In analytic phonics, the cache of memorised sight words is analysed to find the constituent sound–spelling correspondences. (For example, if students have memorised the words 'bag', 'bin' and 'boat', they can analyse these together to see that the grapheme can represent the phoneme /b/.) In analogy phonics, students attempt to decode unknown words through analogous references to the cache of sight words. (For example, if students have memorised the words '<u>b</u>ag' and '<u>red</u>', they can then use the implicit sound–spelling correspondences to decode 'bed'.)

Bottom-up phonics

In bottom-up approaches, the teaching of sound–spelling correspondences begins with the relationships between graphemes and phonemes and then blends these into whole words, though this blending into whole words can, and should, begin immediately. (For example, students may be taught that in the word 'sit', the first grapheme represents a /s/ phoneme, the second represents an /i/ phoneme and the last represents a /t/ phoneme.) This approach to phonics is commonly called **synthetic phonics**.

McGuinness (2006) also draws a distinction between phonics approaches that she terms '**linguistic phonics**' and the rest.[10] The first key difference between linguistic phonics and other approaches is that the former ensures that the teaching of phonics matches the underlying logic of written English, specifically that sounds are represented by spellings, and so the teaching progresses from sound to print, rather than vice versa. Thus, statements like, 'This letter *makes* a /b/ sound', are considered nonsensical, giving children damaging misinformation about how reading works. The second key difference is that linguistic phonics approaches ensure that the teaching of phonics goes far beyond the **initial/basic code** of the most common sound–spelling correspondences and explicitly teaches around 175 sound–spelling correspondences.[11] While all linguistic phonics approaches are examples of synthetic phonics, not all synthetics phonics approaches count as linguistic phonics.

The efficacy of different approaches

Although there is something approaching consensus among reading experts on the value of systematic phonics instruction, there are conflicting claims made about the relative efficacy of the different forms of systematic phonics instruction. Castles, Rastle and Nation (2018) suggested that despite some evidence that synthetic phonics should be preferred, the research findings are not yet overwhelming, and thus the central concern should be that phonics is taught in a systematic fashion, be it via synthetic phonics or another approach.[12] In contrast, Rose (2006) determined that the available evidence *was* strong enough to advocate synthetic phonics as the preferable approach.[13] McGuinness (2006) went further, arguing partly on the basis of a longitudinal study in Scotland's Clackmannanshire County and a study in London's

Docklands that phonics approaches that most closely resembled her 'linguistic phonics prototype' were the most successful. Regardless of these competing claims, the teaching of synthetic phonics was made statutory in local authority maintained English schools in 2006.

It is here that I must make my own opinions on this subject clear. Despite the equivocation of some reading experts on the relative value of synthetic phonics relative to top-down approaches like analytic phonics, I am largely convinced by the underlying logic of a synthetic phonics approach. As there is a consensus on the need for systematic phonics instruction, it is sensible to employ an approach that makes the systematic introduction and revision of sound–spelling correspondences most comprehensible for both teachers and students. Synthetic phonics offers the simplest way to achieve this, and although the evidence for choosing synthetic phonics over top-down phonics instruction may not be considered overwhelming by many at present, there is certainly enough to suggest that it is our best bet while we await further research to better guide our teaching. In addition, I am prone to agree with the logic underpinning linguistic phonics approaches because these make clear to teachers and students how written English actually operates.

Phonemic awareness

One of the challenges of teaching children to read written languages that have phonemes as the basis of their code is that they must learn to identify phonemes in words. This is made all the more challenging by the fact that the idea of physically discrete phonemes within words is an illusion.[14] In reality, the sounds within a spoken word are continuous, and the recognition of individual phonemes within them is a skill both *required for* reading and *developed by* reading.[15] (This was demonstrated by a study of Portuguese adults who could not read. Their ability to recognise and manipulate phonemes was severely lacking compared to similar study participants who had learned to read to a rudimentary level as adults.)[16] This ability to discern discrete phonemes within words is called **phonemic awareness**. (The ability to recognise units of sound within speech more generally – be they phonemes, syllables, whole words, etc. – is called **phonological awareness**. Thus, phonemic awareness is an aspect of phonological awareness.)

McGuinness (2006) encouraged the restriction of phoneme awareness instruction to those skills that were automatically present in synthetic phonics instruction, namely **segmenting** (isolating phonemes in sequence, e.g. 'bet' → /b/ /e/ /t/) and **blending** (joining up phonemes to form a word (e.g. /b/ /e/ /t/ → 'bet').[17] These are the essential components of learning to spell and read. However, some recent evidence has suggested that more advanced training in phonemic awareness can be beneficial for those struggling exceptionally to learn phonics.[18] This training comprises manipulating phonemes, specifically via **phoneme deletion** (What word would remain if we remove the /t/ phoneme from 'stag'?) and **phoneme substitution** (What word would be made if we replace the /t/ phoneme in 'stag' with a /n/ phoneme?). The research in question suggests that these phonemic awareness activities should take place as oral-only activities (i.e. without reference to written words) alongside phonics instruction as a potential intervention. In contrast, other studies suggest that such phoneme manipulation activities are more beneficial when accompanied by words in writing rather than operating as mere oral phonemic manipulation.[19] Either way, there is no current evidence that would suggest that oral-only phoneme manipulation activities should be used as a day-to-day component of phonics programmes.

Sight words

In various phonics programmes, **sight words** form part of the instruction. In the case of top-down phonics approaches (i.e. analytic phonics or analogy phonics), memorising a cache of words by sight is a necessary condition before the actual correspondences between graphemes and phonemes can be learned. In bottom-up approaches (i.e. synthetic phonics), these sight words are often, but not always, included for a different reason. Sight words are often high-frequency words, labelled sometimes as 'tricky words', that appear a great deal in written and spoken English. In some classrooms, they are described accurately as words that require grapheme–phoneme correspondences that the children have not yet learned. In other classrooms, they are inaccurately described as words that *can't* be decoded. The former is obviously preferable to the latter. Regardless, it is common practice for children to be required to memorise these words as whole units through a process of 'repetition and feedback' (p. 15), something which is controversial.[20] Currently, the evidence on the efficacy of whole-word memorisation of a limited number of sight words is far from clear. Some believe that almost any teaching of words by sight is both unnecessary and potentially debilitating.[21] They argue that all words should be introduced via their sound–spelling correspondences, even when the particular correspondences haven't been taught to children yet, a position supported implicitly by the UK Department for Education.[22] Others believe that this position isn't backed up by the available evidence and view the teaching of a selection of words by sight as a useful part of phonics instruction.[23] Still others see there being a compromise between the two positions, in which sight words are introduced and practised initially with reference to the sound–spelling correspondences followed by repeated exposure (i.e. whole-word memorisation) where necessary. My view is that while there isn't clear evidence against the memorisation of a limited number of sight words, the practice contradicts the central message that we must give to children, namely that decoding is how we learn to read. It also contradicts our best theories of word learning processes.[24] I personally advocate teaching all new words via direct reference to their sound–spelling correspondences. Although this means explaining to children that a given phoneme can be represented in more than one way, something which may seem complicated, it sensitises children to the real structure behind written English and how we read. When in doubt, this should be our guiding principle.

Regular and irregular words

Part of the reasoning often given for the teaching of sight words is the concept of 'regular' and 'irregular' words. 'Some words are irregular, so we just have to memorise them', or so goes the argument. However, the regular/irregular dichotomy is a false one.[25] The correspondences between phonemes and graphemes within words exist on a spectrum between those that are very common and those that are used rarely, perhaps only in one word in the entire language. Where a word contains one or more correspondences that aren't part of initial/basic phonics instruction, it is often defined as irregular. For example, <was> is often defined as an irregular word because the <a> grapheme represents the /o/ phoneme. But is this actually irregular? The <a> grapheme represents the /o/ phoneme in many words, some of them quite common (e.g. 'want', 'what', 'swap', 'swan'). The use of regular and irregular to describe words implies an understanding of phonics as only a simple set of one-to-one correspondences with words that match these entirely being regular and those that don't being irregular. A more accurate understanding of phonics solves all this: the graphemes of English can represent more than one phoneme. After the initial/basic code of the most common correspondences has been taught, children must learn the other less common correspondences between graphemes and phonemes. Yes, there are complete oddballs in the language like 'catarrh'. (Given its infrequency in the language, teaching the correspondence between the <arrh> grapheme and the /ar/ phoneme (as in 'bar' or 'tar') almost certainly isn't worth the effort as it only appears in one rarely used word.)[26] Nevertheless, teaching an **advanced code** of correspondences removes any need to refer inaccurately to regular and irregular words.[27]

Letter names

The efficacy of teaching children letter names is also hotly contested. Defenders of the practice point to evidence that the learning of letter names is associated with better reading outcomes.[28] Those who disagree – particularly those that advocate linguistic phonics approaches – argue that this correlation doesn't show us much because children who have learned letter names are more likely to come from homes that value and support the learning of reading. Also, they argue that the teaching of letter names takes valuable teaching time and causes confusion for children.[29] Solity (2003) suggested that the learning of letter names makes more sense *after* children have gained fluency with the initial sound–spelling correspondences of phonics.[30] In the complex reality of classroom practice, however, many children will arrive at school already having learned letter names and so may be confused if teachers do not acknowledge this. My personal view is that one should, ideally, not spend valuable time teaching letter names before the second year of children's schooling, but this should not involve pretending that letter names don't exist with children who have already learned them. As ever, the theory must respect the practical reality of each classroom.

Decodable/phonically controlled books

As implied by the prior discussion of regular and irregular words, the vast majority of words in written English are decodable. Thus, the phrase '**decodable books**' is a misnomer. To be precise, decodable books are those which have been selected to allow children to practise decoding using the sound–spelling correspondences that they have *already been taught*. For this reason, decodable books are better described as phonically controlled books.

As with much of phonics, there is some debate about the use of phonically controlled books. The national curriculum in England states that children in Year 1 (age 5–6) should, 'read aloud accurately books that are consistent with their developing phonic knowledge and that do not require them to use other strategies to work out words' (p. 21).[31] Those generally opposed to systematic phonics teaching often deride these books as artificial or boring. Intriguingly some advocates of systematic phonics believe that the use of phonically controlled books should be minimised.[32] They argue that there is little applied research that supports phonically controlled books, and that the evidence that does exist is mixed.[33] They also argue that learning to read is statistical in that it requires the recognition of patterns through exposure to large quantities of text and that phonically controlled books may hamper this process.

Given the current lack of clarity provided by direct comparisons between children learning with phonically controlled books and those learning *without*, it makes sense to consider the justification for their use and what this entails in practice. Phonically controlled books provide necessary opportunities for children to practise the sound–spelling correspondences that they have learned, without constantly encountering words that force them to guess or seek assistance. It is easy to forget just how frustratingly difficult the initial steps of reading can be for children, particularly those that struggle more than most. Phonically controlled books give children a taste of success, and crucially this success comes as a result of using their newfound decoding skills rather than resorting to picture clues or whole-word guessing. Nevertheless, phonically controlled books also do not entirely prepare children for the reality of reading in which unfamiliar sound–spelling correspondences will inevitably need to be dealt with. If the transition to 'normal' books is not to be demoralisingly abrupt, in their second year of learning to read, children need to be gradually introduced to text that contains more unfamiliar sound–spelling correspondences than they encounter in phonically controlled books. Ideally, this introduction should be carefully supervised by teachers. In this way, if children begin to exhibit strategies other than decoding using learned sound–spelling correspondences, they can once again focus entirely on decodable text. Equally, if they thrive, they can progress to a greater focus on 'real' books and to the statistical learning from reading that they will undertake for the rest of their learning journey. However, this does not mean that phonically controlled books should form no part of their instruction at this point. Practising the sound–spelling correspondences learned in phonics lessons should remain a component of instruction for all children while they learn the most common sound–spelling correspondences.

Does this mean that, in the first year of learning to read in school, children should only *experience* decodable books? Absolutely not. As will be discussed later, it is essential that children are read to and engage in rich discussion of texts from the very beginning of their time in school. Equally, parents/carers can certainly have a positive impact on learning by reading to their children at home. Nevertheless, using the skills learned in phonics lessons – and embedding this as *the* way to decode words – is of paramount importance for those first learning to read, and using phonically controlled texts is the best way to achieve this.

Spelling and retrieval in phonics sessions

Because the aim of phonics instruction is to develop children's ability to decode words, it would be easy to assume that children should spend their time only *decoding* via blending and segmenting words, along with some phonemic manipulation, as described earlier. In fact, the process of *encoding* words (i.e. hearing words aloud and segmenting them in order to spell them) is an essential component of phonics instruction.[34] This can be enhanced further by children saying the sounds as they write the spellings of words.[35]

Along with lots of spelling, a crucial component of phonics instruction is that it thoroughly builds on what has been learned before. All phonics learning needs to be repeatedly retrieved and used in new situations to ensure that children become fluent in their use of the sound–spelling correspondences that they have been taught. One method that is common in classrooms is the use of flashcards to retrieve the most common correspondences between graphemes and phonemes, those relating to the initial/basic code. However, I suspect that this practice is less than ideal. Why? Although this retrieval is valuable, the use of flashcards implies to children that specific graphemes are always related to specific phonemes regardless of the context.

Showing children a <ch> grapheme on an isolated flashcard, and expecting them to recall the /ch/ phoneme may have benefits in terms of developing recall, but it also may confuse them more when they encounter words where the <ch> grapheme represents a /sh/ phoneme, such as in words like 'chef' and 'machine'. The best way for children to meet *and retrieve* sound–spelling correspondences is in the context of words where these correspondences have meaning.[36] Again, where possible, the teaching of phonics should match the logic of our written language. That said, there isn't currently a body of evidence that compares equivalent phonics programmes that use flashcards and those that do not, and – despite my suspicions – it seems unlikely that the use of flashcards has a major impact one way or another.

What if ...?

This is a brief but necessary aside into one of the most common questions asked about phonics instruction: 'If phonics doesn't work for a particular child, what then?' The question itself betrays a certain misunderstanding of what reading is and/or what the aim of phonics instruction is. While there is some evidence to suggest that short-term gains in reading outcomes can be made by supporting older children with reading comprehension strategies, there is no escaping the fact that competence in reading depends on fluent decoding.[37] Fluent decoding in turn depends on a student's knowledge of the common sound–spelling correspondences of English and the skills relating to phonemic awareness. Phonics instruction is the attempt to teach these correspondences and skills. Even if one mistakenly thinks that a child's best chance is to develop their grasp of these connections through self-discovery, this is merely passing the responsibility for phonics instruction from the teacher to the student. If they succeed, it will inevitably be because they have grasped the necessary knowledge and skills for themselves. 'Giving up' on phonics instruction when the knowledge and skills have not been learned by the child is to abandon one's responsibility to teach that child to decode. Yes, there are extreme and exceptionally rare circumstances under which such a decision might be taken, but it shouldn't be taken lightly.

The phonics screening check, non-words and assessment

In England, children are subject to a phonics screening check at the end of Year 1. This brief check of children's decoding skills was introduced against a backdrop of fierce criticism and has proved to be controversial.[38] Since its introduction, some have argued that although the check is valid as a diagnostic tool, it doesn't give information that is not already known by teachers, and that the money spent on its administration could be better spent on improving teachers' understanding of phonics instruction.[39] Others have argued – based on the national data derived from the check – that its use as an accountability tool for schools diminishes its accuracy and utility.[40] The testing of some non-words – also known as 'nonsense words', 'alien words' or 'monster' words' – has also been criticised. (Non-words are words that don't exist in written English such as 'fip' or 'dest' and thus only test a child's ability to decode rather than their recognition of words that might already be familiar to them.) Interestingly, and perhaps revealingly, this criticism has come from both opponents and advocates of the phonics screening check: some opponents argue that non-words could confuse and demoralise readers; some advocates argue that the check should consist entirely of non-words to ensure that the check measures only decoding skills. Regardless of the criticism, the check reflects a welcome focus on the importance of phonics and is – in my experience – administered sensitively by teachers in a way that has no negative impact on children. That said, there are two things of which to be aware as a classroom teacher or a reading coordinator. First, while the use of non-words in the check makes a great deal of sense, this should not mean that children are ever *taught* using non-words.[41] Second, the timing of the phonics check seems to have given some schools the impression that phonics has been 'completed' at the end of Year 1 when in fact the teaching of the advanced code has only just begun at that point. It is often the case that schools view the phonics screening check as the endpoint of their responsibility in tracking children's understanding of phonics. This is unwise. Many children return from the summer holidays before Year 2 having regressed significantly in their understanding of the phonics skills they had seemingly learned. For this reason – and due to the possible inaccuracy of a one-off, five-minute test – *all children's* grasp of phonics should be tracked into Year 2 and beyond, not just those who didn't pass the check and thus will re-take the test at the end of Key Stage 1.

Beyond phonics

The most common straw man argument that is presented as a criticism of systematic phonics instruction is that it crowds out other elements of the teaching of reading. Here it is important to make a distinction between *methods of reading individual words* and *aspects of reading instruction*. Those that criticise phonics instruction as displacing other methods of reading individual words are clinging on to a damaging misconception. Learning to decode is *the* method that children need to grasp and master if they are to become fluent readers. Other methods – such as the cueing systems discussed earlier – are reading fluency dead ends. In contrast, those that criticise phonics instruction as displacing other aspects of reading teaching such as songs, rhymes and stories with rich discussion would have a point, were it the case that (a) anyone were advocating this position, or (b) such displacement had occurred. While I naturally cannot speak for all teachers of young children, I would be surprised to find any teacher that – due to the requirement to teach phonics – had made the egregious error of ceasing to read aloud to children or engage them in rich conversation. From my experience, thinking that such an error is likely would be to grossly underestimate the expertise of those that teach the youngest children.

As implied by the simple view of reading, recognition and use of common sound–spelling correspondences are a necessary but insufficient part of learning to read. From the very beginning of children's formal education as readers, there are multiple aspects of reading that need to be taught consistently and skilfully by teachers who understand how these different aspects interact. The first of these, reading fluency, will be addressed in the next chapter.

——————————————— In a nutshell ... ———————————————

- Understand the logic behind the teaching of an initial/basic code and an advanced code, specifically that each phoneme can be represented by multiple graphemes and that each grapheme can represent multiple phonemes.
- Know that systematic synthetic phonics instruction is harmless to all, beneficial to most and essential for some.
- Avoid anything that discourages decoding as the primary method of dealing with an unknown word, including whole-word guessing and using 'cueing systems'.
- Ensure that developing the crucial skills of blending and segmenting are a substantial component of every phonics lesson.
- Minimise or avoid entirely the teaching of 'sight words' as whole units; where words are introduced and encountered that contain unfamiliar sound–spelling correspondences, make this clear to children (e.g. 'In this word, the /ch/ sound is shown this way ...'); this includes 'high-frequency' or 'tricky' words.
- Understand that the correspondences in all words exist on a spectrum between those that are most common and those that are exceedingly rare, and thus that describing words as 'regular' or 'irregular' doesn't make sense.
- Consider whether the teaching of letter names adds unnecessary confusion for children in your setting in the first year of their formal reading education.
- Ensure that spelling and systematic retrieval of previously taught sound–spelling correspondences is a component of all phonics sessions and that both take place in the context of words (rather than with flashcards with isolated sounds).
- Teach phonics in a manner that is both engaging and ensures that as much time as possible is spent on the key aspects of phonics instruction: learning sound–spelling correspondences in the context of real words, segmenting, blending, manipulating phonemes and spelling (which combines these skills).

(Continued)

- Do not teach non-words, except perhaps very briefly if you need to explain what children will encounter in a phonics screening check.
- Ensure that all phonics teaching is reflective, providing immediate support to those who struggle.
- Persevere with phonics, giving more time for those that need it; genuinely fluent reading is close to impossible without knowledge of sound–spelling correspondences and the skills related to phonemic awareness that are taught explicitly in systematic phonics instruction; know that to abandon phonics instruction is to leave children to learn the necessary knowledge and skills on their own.

Other implications for the classroom

It can be helpful to identify in a discrete fashion the essential knowledge and skills that children need to gain through phonics instruction:

1　They need to learn the sound–spelling correspondences in English, starting with the most common.
2　They need to learn that the roughly 44 sounds of our language are represented with spellings that can comprise one, two, three or four letters.
3　They need to learn that a sound can be represented by different spellings and that a spelling can represent different sounds.
4　They need to learn the phonemic awareness skills of segmenting and blending.

Many of the phonics lessons I have seen do not have enough emphasis on the essential skills of segmenting and blending. Often the majority of such lessons is taken up with activities that only focus on memorising sound–spelling correspondences and 'sight' words. While children's knowledge of sound–spelling correspondences is fundamental, it is a weak grasp of segmenting and blending *using* these sound–spelling correspondences that most commonly slows children's progress. In particular, children tend to struggle most to segment and blend words with adjacent consonant sounds. (A word with a consonant sound, a vowel sound and then a consonant sound is called a CVC word, e.g. 'hen', 'top' or 'pick'. Mono-syllabic words with adjacent consonant sounds can be described as CCV, VCC, CCVC, CVCC, CCCVC, CCVCC and CVCCC words, e.g. 'fly', 'ant', 'flag', 'help', 'splat', 'cramp' and 'gulps'.) Thus, once children have learned some of the initial code with blending and segmenting using CVC words, they then need lots of practice segmenting and blending VCC, CCVC, CVCC, CCCVC, CCVCC and CVCCC words before moving on to new sound-letter correspondences. If the children in a class are still struggling to segment and blend with the sound–spelling correspondences that they have learned, it is best to continue practising these skills before introducing further sound–spelling correspondences.

Phonics is difficult to teach well. The depth of English orthography means that children need systematic instruction that builds incrementally on what has already been learned and teachers need to choose their words carefully to avoid giving children a false impression of how reading works. Where 'sight' words are introduced, it should be made clear that these are not 'words that can't be decoded' and that they are 'tricky' only because particular sound–spelling correspondences haven't yet been learned. Of course, phrases like 'sound–spelling correspondences' are of no use in the classroom, but children can be taught that a given grapheme 'shows' or 'codes' a particular sound. What matters is that the language is consistent and does not build misconceptions, as happens when we describe a given grapheme 'making' a particular sound or a letter as 'silent'.

As with many areas of learning, do not underestimate the value of routines in supporting children to learn. Using the same language and activities to introduce, practise and retrieve given sound–spelling correspondences allows children to focus on the learning at hand rather than on superficial details.

Children will naturally differ in how difficult they find learning to decode. Some will seem to find the learning much easier, especially those from home environments rich in spoken English and where books are plentiful and valued. It is important to re-emphasise that those who struggle – in almost all cases – merely need more time and more practice. It is our job as teachers to find ways to ensure that as many children as possible are given the time they require to learn to decode. In most circumstances, I don't recommend children missing brief components of other learning in order to 'keep up' with an element of their learning deemed to be of greater importance. However, in the case of phonics, I make an exception. For many children, extra time and attention – perhaps as little as an extra 10 per cent each week – can be the difference between thriving as early readers and struggling over the long term. Brief, well-timed extra support is far preferable to the need for significant interventions later in school.

When planning and teaching phonics lessons, consider whether the activities used are efficient. While efficiency might seem quite a dreary metric by which to judge any form of teaching, particularly that undertaken with young children, it is nonetheless central. I have observed too many phonics lessons where 20 minutes is spent spelling a single CVC word in wool. (A CVC word is a word with a consonant sound, a vowel sound and then a consonant sound, e.g. 'deck'.) While this may be a productive activity for developing fine motor control, if the aim of the lesson is to practise using sound–spelling correspondences, then it is a hugely inefficient activity. If in doubt when planning activities, ask yourself this question: 'How much time will the children spend thinking about the learning at hand?'

As discussed above, phonically controlled books (i.e. decodable books) are an essential component of supporting children to embed their grasp of sound–spelling correspondences. For this reason, advocates of phonically controlled books sometimes take extreme positions on their use that don't reflect the underlying evidence or the complex reality of learning to read. It would be easy to come to the conclusion that children in the first two years of school should *never* face a word that doesn't comply with the sound–spelling correspondences that they have already learned. Nevertheless, even the best phonically controlled books introduce children to words with sound–spelling correspondences that they are yet to master, words such as 'the' and 'is'. Yes, children should practise decoding from texts in which the vast majority of words can be decoded using the knowledge they have gained already in phonics lessons. However, within a couple of years, children will face books where some words contain unfamiliar sound–spelling correspondences. Thoughtful use of phonically controlled books within a school should prepare children for this reality. While almost all words in phonically controlled books should be accessible through their phonics knowledge, during the second year of learning to read, it is probably sensible to gradually introduce children to books where an increasing minority of words cannot be entirely decoded. In this way, children are gradually made ready for the complexities of non-phonically controlled books, and they also begin the important process of combining their decoding knowledge with their vocabulary to spot new patterns between spellings and sounds.[42]

Parents/carers are often understandably keen to support their children as they learn to read. It is important that they are supported to appreciate that their children need to practise their decoding in order to become fluent readers. Children will likely develop their decoding skills more rapidly and confidently if they are supported through regular decoding practice at home. This being the case, it can be useful to discuss how phonics is taught with parents/carers at parents' evenings and in information evenings especially undertaken in school on the subject of phonics. Equally, bookmarks can be used to highlight to parents/carers the difference between the phonically controlled books (or other decoding practice material) that children should read *to* their parents/carers and the other books that children may take home that are to be read *by* or *with* their parents/carers.

––––––––––– Questions for professional discussions –––––––––––

- Children initially decode from text that is phonically controlled to allow them to practise using the sound–spelling correspondences that they have learned and to ensure that the concept of decoding is embedded. What downsides might there be to children *only* experiencing phonically controlled text for too long (e.g. the first three years of learning to decode)?
- What might be the issues related to introducing the first few sound–spelling correspondences too quickly? What might be the issues related to introducing the first few sound–spelling correspondences too slowly?

─────────────────── Retrieval quiz ───────────────────

1   What is the difference between top-down and bottom-up phonics approaches?
2   What is the difference between phonemic awareness and phonological awareness?
3   Why is it a false dichotomy to describe words in English as being either regular or irregular?
4   What are the advantages of ensuring children have access to phonically controlled books?
5   Name two types of phonemic manipulation that are essential to phonics instruction.
6   Name two types of phonemic manipulation that are not essential to phonics instruction.

Further reading

- Castles, A., Rastle, K. and Nation, K. (2018). Ending the reading wars: Reading acquisition from novice to expert. *Psychological Science in the Public Interest*, 19(1), 5–51.
- MacKechnie, C., Linguistic Phonics Blog. https://linguisticphonics.wordpress.com.
- McGuinness, D. (2006). *Early Reading Instruction: What Science Really Tells Us About How to Teach Reading*. Cambridge, MA: MIT Press.
- The Reading Ape: www.thereadingape.com.
- Walker, J., The Literacy Blog. https://theliteracyblog.com.

References

1   Castles, A., Rastle, K. and Nation, K. (2018). Ending the reading wars: Reading acquisition from novice to expert. *Psychological Science in the Public Interest*, 19(1), 5–51.
2   McGuinness, D. (2006). *Early Reading Instruction: What Science Really Tells Us About How to Teach Reading*. Cambridge, MA: MIT Press.
3   McGuinness, D. (1997). Decoding strategies as predictors of reading skill: A follow-on study. *Annals of Dyslexia*, 47(1), 115–150.
4   Moats, L. (2019). Phonics and spelling: Learning the structure of language at the word level. In Kilpatrick, D. A., Joshi, R. M. and Wagner, R. K. (eds), *Reading Development and Difficulties*. Cham: Springer International Publishing, 39–62.
5   Ibid.; *Why the Reading Brain Can't Cope with Triple Cueing.* The Reading Ape. Available at: www.thereadingape.com/single-post/2019/01/03/Why-the-reading-brain-cant-cope-with-triple-cueing (accessed 30 November 2020).
6   Ehri, L. C. (1998). Grapheme–phoneme knowledge is essential for learning to read words in English. In Metsala, J. L. and Ehri, L. C. (eds), *Word Recognition in Beginning Literacy*, Mahwah, NJ: Lawrence Erlbaum Associates, 3–40; Rack, J. P., Snowling, M. J. and Olson, R. K. (1992). The nonword reading deficit in developmental dyslexia: A review. *Reading Research Quarterly*, 27, 29–53.

7   *Phonics* (2018). The Education Endowment Foundation, 30 August. Available at: https://educationendowmentfoundation.org.uk/evidence-summaries/teaching-learning-toolkit/phonics/ (accessed 7 January 2021); National Reading Panel (US), National Institute of Child Health, Human Development (US), National Reading Excellence Initiative, National Institute for Literacy (US), United States. Public Health Service, & United States Department of Health (2000). *Report of the National Reading Panel: Teaching children to read: An evidence-based assessment of the scientific research literature on reading and its implications for reading instruction: Reports of the subgroups*. National Institute of Child Health and Human Development, National Institutes of Health.

8   Brady, S. A. (2011). Efficacy of phonics teaching for reading outcomes: Indications from post-NRP research. In Brady, S. A., Braze, D. and Fowler, C. A. (eds), *Explaining Individual Differences in Reading: Theory and Evidence (New Directions in Communication Disorders Research)* New York: Psychology Press, 69–96; Moats (2019).

9   Parker, S. (2018). *Reading Instruction and Phonics: Theory and Practice for Teachers*. Boston, MA: Royce-Kotran Publishing.

10 McGuinness (2006).

11 *English Spellings: A Lexicon*. Sounds-Write. Available at: www.sounds-write.co.uk/sites/soundswrite/uploads/files/49-sounds_write_english_spellings_lexicon.pdf (accessed 30 November 2020); Walker, J. (2016). *Castles in the Air*. The Literacy Blog, 2 July. Available at: https://theliteracyblog.com/2016/07/02/castles-in-the-air/ (accessed 7 January 2021).

12 Castles, Rastle and Nation (2018).

13 Rose, J. (2006). *Independent Review of the Teaching of Early Reading – Final Report*. Available at: https://webarchive.nationalarchives.gov.uk/20100512233640/http://publications.teachernet.gov.uk/eOrderingDownload/0201-2006PDF-EN-01.pdf (accessed 7 January 2021).

14 Seidenberg, M. (2017). *Language at the Speed of Sight: How We Read, Why So Many Can't, and What Can Be Done About It*. New York: Basic Books.

15 Willingham, D. T. (2017). *The Reading Mind: A Cognitive Approach to Understanding How the Mind Reads*. Hoboken, NJ: John Wiley & Sons.

16 Morais, J., Cary, L., Alegria, J. and Bertelson, P. (1979). Does awareness of speech as a sequence of phones arise spontaneously? *Cognition*, 7(4), 323–331.

17 McGuinness (2006).

18 Kilpatrick, D. and O'Brien, S. (2019). Effective prevention and intervention for word-level reading difficulties. In Kilpatrick, D. A., Joshi, R. M. and Wagner, R. K. (eds), *Reading Development and Difficulties*. Cham: Springer International Publishing, 179–212.

19 Moats (2019).

20 Castles, Rastle and Nation (2018), 15; Walker (2016).

21 Walker (2016).

22 *English Appendix 1: Spelling*. The English National Curriculum. Available at: https://assets.publishing.service.gov.uk/government/uploads/system/uploads/attachment_data/file/239784/English_Appendix_1_-_Spelling.pdf (accessed 30 November 2020).

23 Castles, Rastle and Nation (2018); McArthur, G. M., Castles, A., Kohnen, S., Larsen, L., Jones, K., Anandakumar, T., Banales, E. (2015). Sight word and phonics training in children with dyslexia. *Journal of Learning Disabilities*, 24, 391–407; Foorman, B., Beyler, N., Borradaile, K., Coyne, M., Denton, C. A., Dimino, J., … and Keating, B. (2016). *Foundational Skills to Support Reading for Understanding in Kindergarten through 3rd Grade (NCEE*

2016-4008). Washington, DC: National Center for Education Evaluation and Regional Assistance (NCEE), Institute of Education Sciences, U.S. Department of Education.

24 Moats (2019).

25 Walker, J. (2018). *The Ill-Conceived Idea of 'Regular' and 'Irregular' Spelling – A Reprise.* The Literacy Blog, 21 September. Available at: https://theliteracyblog.com/2018/09/21/the-ill-conceived-idea-of-regular-and-irregular-spelling-a-reprise/ (accessed 7 January 2021).

26 McGuinness (2006).

27 Walker, J. (2016). *One Sound Different Spellings – The Sounds-Write Way.* The Literacy Blog, 30 April. Available at: https://theliteracyblog.com/2016/04/30/one-sound-different-spellings-the-sounds-write-way/ (accessed 7 January 2021).

28 National Early Literacy Panel (US) (2008). *Developing Early Literacy: Report of the National Early Literacy Panel: a Scientific Synthesis of Early Literacy Development and Implications of Intervention.* Washington, DC: National Institute for Literacy.

29 Walker, J. (2018). *Advocating the Teaching of Letter Names to Children Just Entering School Is Crass.* The Literacy Blog, 21 September. Available at: https://theliteracyblog.com/2019/06/24/advocating-the-teaching-of-letter-names-to-children-just-entering-school-is-crass/ (accessed 7 January 2021).

30 Solity, J. (2003). Teaching phonics in context: A critique of the National Literacy Strategy. Paper presented at the DfES Seminar, Teaching Phonics in the National Literacy Strategy, University of Warwick, 17 March.

31 Department for Education (2013). *The National Curriculum in England*, 21 Available at: https://assets.publishing.service.gov.uk/government/uploads/system/uploads/attachment_data/file/425601/PRIMARY_national_curriculum.pdf (accessed 30 November 2020).

32 Shanahan, T. (2018). *Should We Teach with Decodable Text?* Shanahan on Literacy, 25 August. Available at: https://shanahanonliteracy.com/blog/should-we-teach-with-decodable-text (accessed 7 January 2021).

33 Mesmer, H. A. (2005). Decodable text and the first grade reader. *Reading and Writing Quarterly*, 2(1), 61–86; Jenkins, J. R., Peyton, J. A., Sanders, E. A. and Vadasy, P. F. (2004). Effects of reading decodable texts in supplemental first-grade tutoring. *Scientific Studies of Reading*, 8(1), 53–85.

34 McGuinness (2006).

35 Mann, T. B., Bushell Jr, D. and Morris, E. K. (2010). Use of sounding out to improve spelling in young children. *Journal of Applied Behavior Analysis*, 43(1), 89–93.

36 Walker, J. (2015). *Why Doesn't the Literacy Blog Advocate the Use of Flash Cards?* The Literacy Blog, 16 May. Available at: https://theliteracyblog.com/2015/05/16/why-doesnt-the-literacy-blog-advocate-the-use-of-flash-cards/ (accessed 7 January 2021).

37 The Education Endowment Foundation (2018). *Phonics*, 30 August. Available at: https://educationendowmentfoundation.org.uk/evidence-summaries/teaching-learning-toolkit/phonics/ (accessed 7 January 2021).

38 *The Guardian* (2012). Phonics checks will not improve reading, 21 June. Available at: www.theguardian.com/education/2012/jun/21/phonics-checks-improve-reading (accessed 7 January 2021).

39 Gilchrist, J. M. and Snowling, M. J. (2018). On the validity and sensitivity of the phonics screening check: erratum and further analysis. *Journal of Research in Reading*, 41(1), 97–105.

40 Whittaker, F. (2016). *Phonics Check Needs a Rethink After Data Shows 'Something Dodgy'*. Schools Week, 7 October. Available at: https://schoolsweek.co.uk/phonics-check-needs-rethink-after-data-shows-something-dodgy/ (accessed 7 January 2021).

41 Walker, J. (2018). *Why We Should Be Using But Not Teaching Nonsense Words*. The Literacy Blog, 18 March. Available at: https://theliteracyblog.com/2018/03/18/why-we-should-be-using-but-not-teaching-nonsense-words/ (accessed 7 January 2021).

42 Stuart, M., Masterson, J., Dixon, M. and Quinlan, P. (1999). Inferring sublexical correspondences from sight vocabulary: Evidence from 6- and 7-year-olds. *The Quarterly Journal of Experimental Psychology: Section A*, 52(2), 353–366.

5

FLUENCY

What is fluency?

Reading **fluency** is a pre-requisite for the comprehension that is the purpose of all reading.[1] Given the origins of the word 'fluency' in the Latin word *fluere* meaning 'flowing', one can imagine the idea of reading fluency as suggesting a natural, continuous stream of words. While there is some truth in this definition, for the purposes of teaching, reading fluency has gained a more precise meaning. Fluent reading is defined by Hudson, Lane and Pullen (2005) as '… accurate reading of connected text, at a conversational rate with appropriate prosody' (p. 702).[2] In other words, reading involves **accuracy**, **automaticity** and **prosody**:[3]

- Accuracy is the ability to decode written words without error. Naturally, all reading, be it aloud or silent, involves the odd stumble, even among the most capable readers. Accurate reading is that in which such errors are rare, if not entirely absent.
- Automaticity is the ability to read quickly and with relative ease. The rate at which a person reads depends not only on their skill, but also on the purposes of their reading and on whether they are reading orally or silently. McGuinness (2006) suggested that reading rates below 90 words correct per minute (WCPM) make it close to impossible for meaning to be processed.[4] For most readers, this is too slow a rate to read with prosody, and thus reading rates above 110 WCPM are likely to be required.
- Prosody is the ability to read in a way that mirrors the sounds of natural spoken language. This includes intonation (the rise and fall in tone), stress (the prominence given to particular syllables, words or phrases) and rhythm. Prosody can seem harder to define (or at least measure) than accuracy or automaticity due to the different ways people talk, but you will know it when you hear it. It sounds, simply, like the reading of a capable adult. However, some have attempted to define different levels of prosody, which can be used to support judgements where necessary.[5]

Although I have outlined separately the three aspects of fluency, it is vital that they are considered as different aspects of the same idea. For example, it would be counter-productive to attempt to increase the reading rate of a student without ensuring that this quicker reading was achieved with appropriate accuracy and prosody. The teaching of reading fluency must consider these elements in concert.[6] It is also important for teachers to understand that reading fluency – and the aspects that constitute it – exists on a spectrum. Thus, while one may talk of fluent or dysfluent readers, these labels are a matter of scale rather than clearly defined states.

Orthographic mapping and the self-teaching hypothesis

Reading fluency is based on the frequent practice of sound–spelling correspondences and phonemic awareness skills that constitute phonics instruction. Children must reach what Ehri (2014) described as the 'full alphabetic phase' (p. 9), where they are applying their knowledge of sound–spelling correspondences across entire words.[7] However, this conscious use of phonics skills is only the first step, though an essential one that requires a great deal of practice. There is some evidence – including that from brain imaging – that there are two neural pathways for reading words in fluent readers: a pathway that relies on decoding for unfamiliar words and another for recognising familiar words as whole units, and that fluency depends on the latter.[8] (There are also computational models that suggest that orthography, phonology and meaning are processed in parallel.)[9] Does this contradict the teaching of phonics? If the recognition of words as whole units potentially contributes to fluent reading, should we not be teaching children to do the same? Absolutely not. Fluent reading is acquired only through repeated decoding; it is this that allows the spellings of words to become 'glued' to the pronunciations already stored in a reader's memory.[10] This process is called **orthographic mapping**.[11] This mirrors Share's (2008) self-teaching hypothesis, which suggests that the main way that we learn to rapidly recognise the spellings of given words is through converting them to their related sounds in our mind.[12] In simple terms, evidence suggests that fluent reading relies on repeated decoding using the exact skills taught in phonics.[13]

Quantity and quality

If fluency is developed through the process of orthographic mapping, then what does this tell us about reading instruction? It implies that while children are developing fluency – something which continues into adulthood but is most pronounced when they first learn to read – they must do *lots of decoding*.[14] This might seem obvious, but many schools seem to pay little attention to this quantitative aspect of reading instruction in their classrooms. (In my experience, children at some schools spend a small fraction of the time decoding text each week compared to those at other schools.) Ideally, children will practise their decoding at home with parents/carers as well as in school, but often this isn't the case. It is the responsibility of schools to ensure that children are doing lots of decoding, especially when they are first developing as readers. (See Chapter 21 for more on the practicalities of this.)

Fluency practice via repeated oral reading

High quantities of decoding with a range of words isn't the only way to enhance a child's reading fluency. Evidence for this lies in the fact that there are two types of slow readers: those who read slowly *due to poor decoding skills* and those who read slowly *despite good decoding skills*.[15] One reason for this can relate to a lack of vocabulary breadth: orthographic mapping (i.e. attaching spellings to their pronunciations) requires that the pronunciations of a given word be already stored in the reader's mind. A narrow vocabulary may impede this process. (See Chapter 11 for more on this.) Another reason is that fluency requires coordination of a few skills, such as decoding, eye movements and quick recall of pronunciations. Fortunately, research strongly suggests that this coordination can be developed through a relatively simple practice: repeated oral reading. Getting children to repeatedly read a short text aloud, while they aim to read it with greater fluency each time, leads to improved fluency over time.[16] This **fluency practice** is strengthened when children, most of the time, are provided with a modelled reading of the same text to guide their attempts.[17] Fluency practice can also be strengthened by ensuring that the text used is above the level of difficulty that the children would otherwise attempt to read.[18] Repeated oral reading can take place with children reading aloud to one another, following modelling from a teacher. While one aim is to develop fluency in this way, it is essential that children see the underlying aim of all reading practice as the derivation of meaning from text, and this should inform how fluency practice is undertaken.[19] (See Chapter 21 for more on the practicalities of fluency practice.)

Some argue that fluency practice is best undertaken with texts that lend themselves to performance – particularly poetry, songs and speeches – and there is some evidence that fluency practice of this sort is productive.[20] Nevertheless, noticing and using punctuation, something often used inconsistently in poetry and songs, is a key aspect of reading, one that emphasises the phrase and clause boundaries that children need to recognise to support their prosody. (Experienced classroom teachers all know that dysfluent readers often take little notice of punctuation.) Until definitive research is available, it would appear to be far more sensible to undertake repeated oral reading with a wide variety of text types, with a slightly greater emphasis on poetry, songs and speeches. Where a class of children are evidently competent in the use of punctuation in reading but lack prosodic rhythm, it may be beneficial to use these types of texts to a greater extent. As with all aspects of teaching reading, thoughtful text choice that reflects the needs of each unique class of children is a powerful tool at the teacher's disposal.

It is also important to know which methods do *not* support the development of fluency. There is insufficient evidence to suggest that silent reading supports the development of initial reading fluency – though it is obviously beneficial in other ways once children are fluent enough to independently construct meaning as they read.[21] Accurate decoding, silent or otherwise, does contribute to the development of orthographic mapping, which enhances fluency over the longer term. Nevertheless, while children's reading is still dysfluent, classroom time dedicated to silent reading is time that could be better spent. In addition, the utility of fluency practice is undermined by texts that are so short or repetitive that children can quickly memorise them.[22] To reiterate, fluency practice should take place through repeated oral reading of challenging, unmemorisable texts with modelling and guidance from a teacher.

Early fluency skills: concept of word

Given that one aspect of fluent reading is automatic decoding, it would seem to make little sense to try to develop fluency *before* children are ready to decode sentences. Nevertheless, this is not the case. There is hidden knowledge that is required for reading fluency that we often take for granted, such as knowledge of the print orientation in English (left to right and down the page). Another essential idea that children must grasp is the **concept of word**, which is the awareness of words as units of spoken and written language. Research indicates that children often arrive at school unaware that speaking can be divided into individual words or unsure of what the term 'word' even means.[23] In addition, some studies suggest that children's ability to recognise words as individual units in text plays a lynchpin role in their reading development, allowing them to 'freeze-frame' a word to analyse its phonemes.[24] The reading of basic sentences in phonics instruction supports the development of children's concept of word. Some reading experts also advocate a process called 'finger-point reading', where children point at words as a teacher reads a text aloud, one that the children have partly or entirely memorised.[25] However, there is a danger that finger-point reading implicitly encourages children to view reading as the memorisation of words as whole units or the decoding of initial letters followed by guesswork. Fortunately, there is an alternative. When a teacher reads aloud to the class each day, by occasionally showing the class the movement of his/her finger from word to word as he/she reads, he/she develops the children's concept of word without risk to their grasp of what reading entails. The teacher also embeds the children's understanding of print orientation in English. (See Chapter 21 for more on this.)

Assessment of fluency

A student's level of reading fluency is closely correlated with their ability to comprehend meaning from text, the ultimate goal of reading.[26] Although some dysfluent readers develop compensatory strategies – and some fluent readers pay too little attention to comprehension – an assessment of fluency still provides a valuable insight into the reading ability of a child at a given moment, suggesting potential adaptations to classroom teaching and intervention.[27] (See Chapters 19 and 21 for more on this.) Fluency assessments tend to work by measuring the number of words a child reads correctly in a minute with an age-appropriate text and coupling this with a judgement of their prosody. (Of course, any speech impediments should be sensitively taken into account when administering reading fluency tests and assessing the prosody of a child.) The words correct per minute (WCPM) score can be compared to the benchmarks developed by Hasbrouck and Tindal (2006) to give a norm-referenced view of a student's progress.[28] The DIBELS tests for oral reading fluency are freely available and provide appropriate texts and simple instructions for administering an assessment of fluency.[29] (As Hasbrouck and Tindal's benchmarks and DIBELS assessment materials are both produced in the USA to match specific grades, care must be taken to ensure that ages are converted to allow accurate use and interpretation, e.g. Grade 1 in the US is equivalent to Year 2 in the UK.) At a minimum, fluency assessments should be undertaken twice a year with any student who hasn't yet reached a level of fluency that allows for confident independent reading (specifically 110+ WCPM with 99+ per cent accuracy and appropriate prosody).

————————————— In a nutshell … —————————————

- Ensure that the quantity of decoding done by children each week in reading sessions is part of the conversation in your school about what constitutes effective reading instruction; understand that this has an influence on children's orthographic mapping, which eventually allows words to be processed rapidly.
- Use a significant proportion of your reading sessions to develop children's reading fluency via repeated oral reading of challenging texts, especially as their decoding fluency first begins to develop between the ages of 6 and 10 years old; ensure all three aspects of fluency – accuracy, automaticity and prosody – are developed through such teaching. (See Chapter 21 for more on this.)

(Continued)

- While they are first learning to decode, develop children's concept of word by sometimes showing how a finger can track words as you read aloud to children.
- Assess children's reading fluency at least twice per year; standardised materials such as DIBELS assessments and age-related oral reading fluency norms can support this.

Other implications for the classroom

More than perhaps any other aspect of reading instruction, fluency practice requires the development of productive routines and astute observation of children's interactions. Children will be required to read to one another, to listen to each other and to follow the words in a text as their partner reads. Making this work requires the instilling of routines and clearly modelling how repeated oral reading should take place. Expectations need to be made explicit in minute detail, ideally ones that are matched in classrooms across the school. Children need to know exactly what to do if they and their partner have finished the text three times or what to do if they cannot decode a word. Simple rules for fluency practice are a must. For example, a set of rules might look like this:

1   The reader reads while the listener follows with a ruler.
2   Let the reader try to decode the word. If they can't and the listener can, the listener can help after the reader has had a go.
3   If neither the reader nor the decoder can decode the word, write it on a whiteboard for sharing with the teacher.
4   Swap roles at the end of the paragraph and start again.
5   Keep taking turns until the timer finishes/the teacher rings the bell, etc.

In my experience of undertaking fluency practice with children in every year group from Year 2 to Year 6, you will be surprised by (a) how much teachers need to sweat the small details when they first get started, and (b) how automated fluency practice can become, though this usually takes at least a couple of weeks. I recommend sitting children in mixed ability pairs and not being afraid to tinker with the seating plan, changing it frequently to keep things fresh. Where necessary, ensure that the stronger decoders go first so they can support the practice of their partners. At first, be intentionally visible to all children and circulate the room to ensure that they are keeping on track. However, as children become more adept at fluency practice, begin to take the opportunity to support the fluency practice of struggling children, perhaps supporting them for longer periods as the rest of the class become more accustomed to the routines of fluency practice.

The modelling of fluent reading is an important aspect of fluency practice, but it takes judgement. While the children do need to hear clear prosody modelled to them for the text they are about to read, I would advise that you read texts aloud at a speed that is slightly slower than you might normally use, without hampering the prosody of your natural speech. Make a conscious effort to read clearly, to give slightly longer emphasis to the gaps between sentences denoted by punctuation and perhaps even to gently accentuate the natural rhythms and changes in tone in your voice. Children should be given every chance to hear what is being read and to experience fluent reading that is calm and not rushed.

As discussed further in Chapter 21, the performance aspect of fluency practice is essential. It ensures that children strive towards a more fluent reading of the text, giving each minute of the session a sense of purpose. Consider introducing this aspect with just student volunteers at first and only once children are comfortable with the routines of the rest of the lesson. Be very cautious in doling out lots of praise for fluent reading as this will likely serve to add unnecessary pressure to those who cannot yet meet that standard. Reading aloud in front of peers can feel very high stakes for a child. In my experience, taking pains to show that this is just another part of the lesson – and *not* an opportunity for a child to impress you – leads to better engagement from the whole class, particularly those that take a little longer to develop reading fluency. A focus on improvement secured during the lesson and a warm 'thank you' to the child who has read aloud is more than enough.

Once the routines of fluency practice are established in your classroom (or ideally across the school), the session itself may not take a large amount of planning, beyond a consideration of the discussion of the text towards the end of the session. This being the case, it can be useful to use planning time to write the texts used for fluency practice, especially for children further down the school. (As fluency practice involves repeated reading, this may only be seven or eight sentences long.) These can match the content from across the curriculum that children are learning, meaning that a fluency practice session supports the children's learning of science, history, etc. Occasionally, consider choosing or writing texts that relate to interests of the class, something that again demonstrates to them that this fluency practice, like all reading, still has the derivation of meaning at its heart.

--------------------- Questions for professional discussions ---------------------

- Is fluency practice an aspect of reading that could be shared with parents/carers to occasionally be undertaken at home? What might be the advantages or disadvantages of this in your setting?
- How could a school ensure that the assessment of fluency did not become misinterpreted as being all about speed? What might be the consequences if this *did* occur?

──────────────── Retrieval quiz ────────────────

1   What are the three aspects of fluency defined in this chapter?
2   What is orthographic mapping and what does it imply about reading instruction?
3   What is 'concept of word' and how might it be developed in children just becoming accustomed to text?
4   What assessments are freely available that can be used to assess children's reading fluency?

Further reading

- Ehri, L. C. (2014). Orthographic mapping in the acquisition of sight word reading, spelling memory, and vocabulary learning. *Scientific Studies of Reading*, 18(1), 5–21.
- Fuchs, L. S., Fuchs, D., Hosp, M. K. and Jenkins, J. R. (2001). Oral reading fluency as an indicator of reading competence: A theoretical, empirical, and historical analysis. *Scientific studies of reading*, 5(3), 239–256.
- Kilpatrick, D. A., Joshi, R. M. and Wagner, R. K. (eds) (2019). *Reading Development and Difficulties*. Cham: Springer International Publishing.
- Shanahan, T., Shanahan on Literacy Blog. https://shanahanonliteracy.com/blog.

References

1   Pikulski, J. J. and Chard, D. J. (2005). Fluency: Bridge between decoding and reading comprehension. *The Reading Teacher*, 58(6), 510–519.
2   Hudson, R. F., Lane, H. B. and Pullen, P. C. (2005). Reading fluency assessment and instruction: What, why, and how? *The Reading Teacher*, 58(8), 702–714.
3   Seidenberg, M. (2017). *Language at the Speed of Sight: How We Read, Why So Many Can't, and What Can Be Done About It*. New York: Basic Books.
4   McGuinness, D. (2006). *Early Reading Instruction: What Science Really Tells Us About How to Teach Reading*. Cambridge, MA: MIT Press.
5   National Center for Education Statistics (2002). *NAEP – Oral Reading Fluency Scale*. Available at: https://nces.ed.gov/nationsreportcard/studies/ors/scale.aspx (accessed 30 November 2020); Kuhn, M. R., Schwanenflugel, P. J. and Meisinger, E. B. (2010). Aligning theory and assessment of reading fluency: Automaticity, prosody, and definitions of fluency. *Reading Research Quarterly*, 45(2), 230–251.
6   Rasinski, T. (2006). Reading fluency instruction: Moving beyond accuracy, automaticity, and prosody. *The Reading Teacher*, 59(7), 704–706.
7   Ehri, L. C. (2014). Orthographic mapping in the acquisition of sight word reading, spelling memory, and vocabulary learning. *Scientific Studies of Reading*, 18(1), 5–21.
8   Taylor, J. S. H., Rastle, K. and Davis, M. H. (2013). Can cognitive models explain brain activation during word and pseudoword reading? A meta-analysis of 36 neuroimaging studies. *Psychological Bulletin*, 139(4), 766.

9   Harm, M. W. and Seidenberg, M. S. (2004). Computing the meanings of words in reading: Cooperative division of labor between visual and phonological processes. *Psychological Review*, 111(3), 662.

10 Miles, K. P. and Ehri, L. C. (2019). Orthographic mapping facilitates sight word memory and vocabulary learning. In Kilpatrick, D. A., Joshi, R. M. and Wagner, R. K. (eds), *Reading Development and Difficulties*. Cham: Springer International Publishing, 63–82.

11 Ehri, L. C. (1992). Reconceptualizing the development of sight word reading and its relationship to recoding. In P. B. Gough, L. C. Ehri and R. Treiman (eds), Reading Acquisition. Mahwah, NJ: Lawrence Erlbaum Associates, 107–143; Ehri (2014).

12 Share, D. L. (2008). Orthographic learning, phonological recoding, and self-teaching. *Advances in Child Development and Behavior*, 36, 31; Miles and Ehri (2019).

13 Yurovsky, D., Fricker, D. C., Yu, C. and Smith, L. B. (2014). The role of partial knowledge in statistical word learning. *Psychonomic Bulletin & Review*, 21(1), 1–22.

14 Stanovich, K. E. and West, R. F. (1989). Exposure to print and orthographic processing. *Reading Research Quarterly*, 402–433.

15 McGuinness (2006).

16 Stahl, S. A. and Kuhn, M. R. (2002). Center for the Improvement of Early Reading Achievement: Making it sound like language: Developing fluency. *The Reading Teacher*, 55(6), 582–584; National Reading Panel (US), National Institute of Child Health, Human Development (US), National Reading Excellence Initiative, National Institute for Literacy (US), United States. Public Health Service, & United States Department of Health (2000). *Report of the National Reading Panel: Teaching children to read: An evidence-based assessment of the scientific research literature on reading and its implications for reading instruction: Reports of the subgroups.* National Institute of Child Health and Human Development, National Institutes of Health; McGuinness (2006).

17 Chard, D. J., Vaughn, S. and Tyler, B. J. (2002). A synthesis of research on effective interventions for building reading fluency with elementary students with learning disabilities. *Journal of Learning Disabilities*, 35(5), 386–406.

18 Padeliadu, S. and Giazitzidou, S. (2018). A synthesis of research on reading fluency development: Study of eight meta-analyses. *European Journal of Special Education Research*, 3(1), 232–256; Shanahan, T. (2017). *How to Teach Fluency So It Takes*. Shanahan on Literacy, 17 September. Available at: https://shanahanonliteracy.com/blog/how-to-teach-fluency-so-that-it-takes (accessed 7 January 2021).

19 Rasinski, T. V. (2012). Why reading fluency should be hot! *The Reading Teacher*, 65(8), 516–522.

20 Rasinski, T. V., Rupley, W. H., Pagie, D. D. and Nichols, W. D. (2016). Alternative Text Types to Improve Reading Fluency for Competent to Struggling Readers. *International Journal of Instruction*, 9(1), 163–178.

21 National Reading Panel (2000).

22 Wolf, G. M. (2018). Developing reading automaticity and fluency: Revisiting what reading teachers know, putting confirmed research into current practice. *Creative Education*, 9(06), 838.

23 Flanigan, K. (2007). A concept of word in text: A pivotal event in early reading acquisition. *Journal of Literacy Research*, 39(1), 37–70.

24   Bowling, E. C. and Cabell, S. Q. (2019). Developing readers: Understanding concept of word in text development in emergent readers. *Early Childhood Education Journal*, 47(2), 143–151.

25   Shanahan, T. (2020). *First You Have to Teach Them to Be Disfluent Readers*. Shanahan on Literacy, 20 June. Available at: https://shanahanonliteracy.com/blog/first-you-have-to-teach-them-to-be-disfluent-readers (accessed 7 January 2021); Ehri, L. C. and Sweet, J. (1991). Fingerpoint-reading of memorized text: What enables beginners to process the print? *Reading Research Quarterly*, 26(4), 442–462.

26   Fuchs, L. S., Fuchs, D., Hosp, M. K. and Jenkins, J. R. (2001). Oral reading fluency as an indicator of reading competence: A theoretical, empirical, and historical analysis. *Scientific Studies of Reading*, 5(3), 239–256.

27   Walczyk, J. J. and Griffith-Ross, D. A. (2007). How important is reading skill fluency for comprehension? *The Reading Teacher*, 60(6), 560–569.

28   Hasbrouck, J. and Tindal, G. A. (2006). Oral reading fluency norms: A valuable assessment tool for reading teachers. *The Reading Teacher*, 59(7), 636–644.

29   University of Oregon. *UO DIBELS Data System*. Available at: https://dibels.uoregon.edu/assessment/index/material/ (accessed 30 November 2020).

Part III
Language Comprehension

6

LANGUAGE COMPREHENSION ≠ LISTENING COMPREHENSION

As we saw in Chapter 2, according to the simple view of reading, decoding and language comprehension together account for all aspects of reading comprehension:

Reading Comprehension (RC) = Decoding (D) × Language Comprehension (LC)

It is tempting to assume that the language comprehension in this equation is synonymous with the listening comprehension that comes naturally to children as long as they are exposed to a rich spoken-language environment.[1] Indeed, people's spoken language skills and reading comprehension tend to be very closely correlated and mutually reinforcing, especially once the reader's decoding has passed a basic level.[2] Speech is also accurately described as the start point for grasping orthography, and there is early evidence that interventions that target oral language in young children lead to improvements in the skills that support reading comprehension.[3] Nevertheless, listening comprehension and the language comprehension described in the simple view of reading are *not* the same thing. This is due to the differences between spoken language and written text.[4] Written text is devoid of the rhythm, intonation and facial expressions of spoken language, with typographic features such as italics providing scant replacement. Written text is also generally more formal and syntactically complex, containing more embedded clauses and other relatively elaborate constructions. Fewer words are used in writing to embed speech in its immediate context, and the pace of comprehension is set by the reader. In contrast, spoken language is more likely

to contain words that embed it in its immediate context, and the pace of comprehension is set by the reader, who can re-read sections and change speed to suit their
reading goals. In short, while *listening comprehension* is a crucial aspect of children's
language capabilities and thus their ability to read, *language comprehension* is a considerably more complex entity, consisting of listening comprehension *and* the aspects of
comprehension that are uniquely required to gain meaning from written texts.

When a class of children are first taught to read, it is the differences between
children's decoding that accounts for most of the differences in their reading capability. However, as they pass the threshold of relatively fluent decoding, the aspects
of language comprehension become increasingly influential in predicting a child's
ability to read. All of these aspects will be discussed in the coming chapters.

———————————————— In a nutshell … ————————————————

- Support children's listening comprehension through the shared enjoyment and rich
  discussion of books, poetry and songs.
- Recognise that listening comprehension and language comprehension in reading,
  though related, are not the same thing and that children will need to be taught the
  unique aspects of the latter.

Other implications for the classroom

While listening comprehension and the language comprehension described in the simple view of reading are not identical, this is not to say that developing children's listening comprehension is not an essential component of reading instruction. On the
contrary, reading to children and discussing the text is an essential component of reading
instruction, especially at the earliest stages. This will develop the vocabulary breadth that
children will require for orthographic mapping (see Chapters 5 and 11) and their understanding of text structure, sentence structure and background knowledge (see Chapters
10 and 12). Just as importantly, sharing books, poetry and songs with young children is
one of the great privileges of being a teacher, something that can, and should, bring joy
to a class and help to inculcate a love of reading and an appreciation of language.

———————————— Questions for professional discussions ————————————

- Beyond the sharing of stories, poetry and songs, how else might listening comprehension be developed in the classroom?
- What might be the impact of weak listening comprehension ability on the motivation
  of a child over the long term?

———————————————————— Retrieval quiz ————————————

1 Name three differences between listening comprehension and the language comprehension involved in reading a text.
2 Why does language comprehension, relative to reading fluency, become a more influential predictive factor of reading ability as children progress through school?

References

1 Castles, A., Rastle, K. and Nation, K. (2018). Ending the reading wars: Reading acquisition from novice to expert. *Psychological Science in the Public Interest*, 19(1), 5–51; Pinker, S. (2009). *Language Learnability and Language Development*. Cambridge, MA: Harvard University Press.

2 Seidenberg, M. (2017). *Language at the Speed of Sight: How We Read, Why So Many Can't, and What Can Be Done About It*. New York: Basic Books; Catts, H. W. and Hogan, T. P. and Adolf, S. M. (2005). Developmental changes in reading and reading disabilities. In Catts, H. W. and Kamhi, A. G. (eds), *The Connections Between Language and Reading Disabilities*. New York: Psychology Press, 25–40; Huettig, F. and Pickering, M. J. (2019). Literacy advantages beyond reading: Prediction of spoken language. *Trends in Cognitive Sciences*, 23(6), 464–475.

3 Moats, L. (2019). Phonics and spelling: Learning the structure of language at the word level. In Kilpatrick, D. A., Joshi, R. M. and Wagner, R. K. (eds), *Reading Development and Difficulties*. Cham: Springer International Publishing, 39–62; Fricke, S., Bowyer-Crane, C., Haley, A. J., Hulme, C. and Snowling, M. J. (2013). Efficacy of language intervention in the early years. *Journal of Child Psychology and Psychiatry*, 54(3), 280–290.

4 Oakhill, J., Cain, K. and Elbro, C. (2014). *Understanding and Teaching Reading Comprehension: A Handbook*. London: Routledge; Montag, J. L., Jones, M. N. and Smith, L. B. (2015). The words children hear: Picture books and the statistics for language learning. *Psychological Science*, 26(9), 1489–1496; Shanahan, T. (2020). *Why Following the Simple View May Not Be Such a Good Idea*. Shanahan on Literacy, 7 March. Available at: https://shanahanonliteracy.com/blog/why-following-the-simple-view-may-not-be-such-a-good-idea (accessed 7 January 2021).

7

SITUATION MODELS

What is comprehension?

I have read to children *The Iron Man* by Ted Hughes at least five times through my career as a teacher. I am fairly confident that I could retell the story over the space of half an hour or so in a way that would give a decent approximation of the plot and characters, though no doubt lacking the lyrical beauty of the original. Despite this, I cannot recall any of the sentences from the story word-for-word, beyond the first couple perhaps. This reveals something important about reading comprehension, something of which you are no doubt already aware, but that is worth saying anyway: as we read, we forget the exact wording of a text and remember an overall representation of the meaning that we have derived from it.[1] This isn't just true after we have finished reading. We mentally construct and update a model of what we have understood from a text while we are in the process of reading it.[2] This view sees the language in a text less as something to be stored directly and more as instructions on how to create a mental representation of the situation being described.[3] This is sometimes described as a **situation model**.[4]

Let's explore this idea a little further using an example. Consider this story opening:

> *Cindy Katz entered the court and strode with confidence towards the baseline, feeling like a different woman to the one she had been moments before. Each Saturday afternoon with her top-of-the-range racket in her grasp, this gentle vicar transformed temporarily into a snarling, remorseless competitor with an almost entirely deserved reputation for terrorising umpires.*

According to the theory behind situation models, as readers we set up a 'token' for Cindy Katz as she is introduced, something that I will represent as a mind map (Figure 7.1).

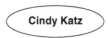

Figure 7.1 'Token' for Cindy Katz

This token is updated as more information is received about Cindy and we associate this information with her (Figure 7.2).

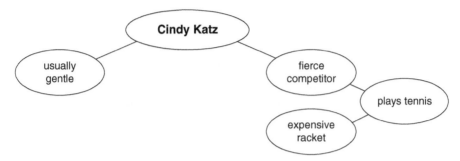

Figure 7.2 Cindy Katz basic situation model

The act of creating and updating a situation model naturally places a strain on our memory. However, differences in our memory are not the only factor that supports or hinders our use of a situation model. Note that in this case the situation model can only be updated effectively if we are able to discern that *'a different woman'*, *'she'*, *'this gentle vicar'* and *'snarling, remorseless competitor'* all refer to the same person. Equally, the situation model is severely diminished if we don't know that *'court'*, *'baseline'*, *'racket'* and *'umpires'* are almost certainly referring to tennis (or another racket sport). Our ongoing grasp of the text relies on our knowledge of the world, specifically that which is related to the situation being described; it also relies on the breadth and depth of our vocabulary, including our knowledge of the functions of articles, prepositions, pronouns, conjunctions, etc. As a text progresses further, it becomes equally important that we can update our situation model by relinquishing the details that are deemed less important while maintaining those that are essential. This is easier to do if we have knowledge of the typical features of a given text structure. In this snippet of narrative, for example, it seems likely that the author wants us to know that Cindy is a gentle character, but with a hidden competitive steel. It is probably less important that Cindy is willing to spend money on expensive things although this is also revealed in the text, and so over time this may be removed from our situation model (Figure 7.3).

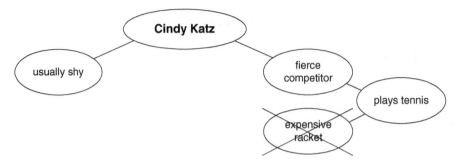

Figure 7.3   Cindy Katz basic situation model – updated

As with our background knowledge and our vocabulary, our experience of narrative exposition helps guide our ongoing understanding.

In Figure 7.3, I have attempted to visually represent an extremely basic situation model for a single character. In reality, an integrated situation model is needed for all of the aspects of a text deemed pertinent. (In the case of a story, this is likely to include characters, setting, plot, themes, etc.) Comprehension can thus be seen as an active process of constructing and updating a situation model of the ideas expressed by a writer. It involves taking the words of a text and creating meaning through a process of personalisation, prioritisation and integration. Assuming we can decode fluently, our ability to use such a model is defined by our understanding of the text's structure; our grasp of the words, phrases and syntax (the order of words to create meaning); and our worldly knowledge of the context being described. All of these will be discussed in greater detail in the coming chapters.

Comprehension skills – a poor use of time

You may have noticed that the factors that underpin a reader's ability to construct and update a situation model – i.e. their language comprehension abilities – are all related to the specifics of whatever text is being read: the text structure knowledge that supports comprehension is the text structure of *that* text; the vocabulary required is the vocabulary of *that* text; the worldly knowledge required is that which relates directly to *that* text. So, is language comprehension a skill that can be transferred to a different context? No, it is not.[5] In my experience, language comprehension teaching often comprises attempts to teach generic skills: explaining main ideas, summarising texts, making inferences, making predictions, etc. It is based on the notion that as long as children practise, say, making an inference in a given context, this will improve their ability to make inferences in other contexts. There is zero evidence to support the existence of such generic comprehension skills, and yet 'doing inference on Mondays' or 'doing prediction in week four of each term' continues to be standard practice in many schools. Much teaching of comprehension resembles what it secretly is: ill-conceived preparation over many years for an end-of-school assessment that, in reality, is largely a measure of a child's reading fluency and their knowledge of vocabulary and the world. Nowhere is the insidious effect of teaching to the test more widespread and more counter-productive than in the teaching of comprehension. We can do better.

Comprehension strategies – a good use of a little time

In contrast to the teaching of generic comprehension *skills*, there is a substantial body of evidence to back up the brief teaching of various **comprehension *strategies***. These strategies, which will be discussed in the coming chapters, tend to be best thought of as a set of tricks that are quickly taught and do not develop further with extensive practice. (It is this which defines them as strategies rather than skills.) While some dispute their value at all, the majority of reading experts accept that the teaching of certain strategies for short periods leads to improved comprehension.[6] These strategies function by ensuring children are aware of their own thinking as they read and of the need to keep track of their own understanding and to connect ideas. As such, the brief teaching of comprehension strategies can be thought of as **metacognition** (i.e. thinking about thinking) for reading, where a strategy is explained, modelled, scaffolded and then applied independently by students.[7] Some argue that a strategies approach that explicitly develops children's metacognition around reading is in conflict with an approach that focuses primarily on the content of a text, but this certainly does not have to be the case, nor should it be.[8] The ways in which different strategies can be used to complement a content-focused approach will be discussed over the coming chapters.

––––––––––––––––––––––––– In a nutshell … –––––––––––––––––––––––––

- Understand the concept of a situation model as something constructed and updated as a reader keeps track of the meaning in a text.
- Know that there are multiple factors to language comprehension and that these factors are *not* generic, transferable skills to be taught through practice in answering certain question types.

Other implications for the classroom

Situation models are a useful representation of what is occurring when a reader grasps the meaning of a text. Nevertheless, having been introduced to the sort of diagrams shown above, it would be easy to believe that they are an accurate representation of what is going on in a person's mind as they read. They are not, nor could they ever be. Even the words we use to attempt to describe how humans learn are woefully inadequate. Day-to-day teaching relies on our acceptance that such descriptions of the learning process are merely tools and that aspects of reading comprehension that we see in the classroom will confound any model of reading comprehension, regardless of how useful it is most of the time.

The difficulty of teaching reading comprehension has led to several attempts to simplify the process, often involving catchy acronyms. In most cases, these attempts reflect what educators *hope* will work based on the usual contents of end-of-school assessments, rather than any reflection of what is known about the process of learning to comprehend. It suffices to say that the core of all reading instruction – once children are relatively fluent decoders – involves encountering and interpreting text, and lots of it. This being the case, there is always a balance to be struck between the amount of time that is spent reading text and the amount of time spent considering deep questions about the text and answering them, perhaps in writing. The challenge for teachers is that the former leaves little to no trail for those who wish to see the 'evidence' of learning (as if such a thing were possible) while the latter produces something tangible and superficially measurable. For this reason, it is tempting to feel that every reading lesson requires something (anything!) written in books. While the answering of questions in writing can indeed be of great value in getting children to reflect on their understanding of a text, remember that it is perfectly possible to teach a productive reading lesson where nothing whatsoever is written down by the students.

―――――――――――― Questions for further discussion ――――――――――――

1   To what extent is the creation of a situation model during reading comprehension, as visualised above, similar to other forms of learning? What might be the differences and similarities?
2   Why might it be the case that reading lessons commonly come to resemble rehearsal for assessments? What are the motivational drivers of this?

―――――――――――――――― Retrieval quiz ――――――――――――――――

1   In this chapter, the creation of situation models for reading comprehension are described as relying on a process of 'personalisation, prioritisation and integration'. Explain what each of these three words means in this context.
2   What is the difference between comprehension skills and comprehension strategies?
3   Comprehension strategies are described as involving 'metacognition for reading'. What is meant by this?

Further reading

- Kintsch, W., Welsch, D., Schmalhofer, F. and Zimny, S. (1990). Sentence memory: A theoretical analysis. *Journal of Memory and Language*, 29(2), 133–159.
- Willingham, D. T. (2017). *The Reading Mind: A Cognitive Approach to Understanding How the Mind Reads*. Hoboken, NJ: John Wiley & Sons.
- Zwaan, R. A. and Radvansky, G. A. (1998). Situation models in language comprehension and memory. *Psychological Bulletin*, 123(2), 162.

References

1 Willingham, D. T. (2017). *The Reading Mind: A Cognitive Approach to Understanding How the Mind Reads*. Hoboken, NJ: John Wiley & Sons.

2 Beck, I. L. and McKeown, M. G. (2002). Questioning the author: Making sense of social studies. *Educational Leadership*, 59(3), 44–47.

3 Zwaan, R. A. and Radvansky, G. A. (1998). Situation models in language comprehension and memory. *Psychological Bulletin*, 123(2), 162.

4 Kintsch, W., Welsch, D., Schmalhofer, F. and Zimny, S. (1990). Sentence memory: A theoretical analysis. *Journal of Memory and Language*, 29(2), 133–159.

5 Liben, D. (2020). The importance of vocabulary and knowledge in comprehension. In Patterson, J. (ed.), *The SAT® Suite and Classroom Practice: English Language Arts/ Literacy*. New York: College Board, 53–69; Willingham, D. T. and Lovette, G. (2014). Can reading comprehension be taught. *Teachers College Record*, 116, 1–3; Shanahan, T. (2018). *Comprehension Skills or Strategies – Is There a Difference and Does It Really Matter?* Shanahan on Literacy, 19 May. Available at: https://shanahanonliteracy.com/ blog/comprehension-skills-or-strategies-is-there-a-difference-and-does-it-matter (accessed 7 January 2021).

6 McGuinness, D. (2006). *Early Reading Instruction: What Science Really Tells Us About How to Teach Reading*. Cambridge, MA: MIT Press; *Comprende? Reading Comprehension – A Skill To Be Taught?* The Reading Ape. Available at: www. thereadingape.com/single-post/2019/06/23/Comprende-Reading-comprehension-a-skill-to-be-taught (accessed 30 November 2020).

7 Quigley, A., Muijs, D. and Stringer, E. (2018). *Metacognition and Self-Regulated Learning: Guidance Report*. Education Endowment Foundation. Available at: https:// educationendowmentfoundation.org.uk/public/files/Publications/Metacognition/EEF_ Metacognition_and_self-regulated_learning.pdf (accessed 7 January 2021).

8 McKeown, M. G., Beck, I. L. and Blake, R. G. (2009). Rethinking reading comprehension instruction: A comparison of instruction for strategies and content approaches. *Reading Research Quarterly*, 44(3), 218–253.

8

COMPREHENSION MONITORING

Research suggests that there are a number of differences between those who comprehend well as they read and those who do not. Although the differences in an individual child can be related to a number of factors (including decoding ability, as seen from the simple view of reading), one key difference on average between good comprehenders and poor comprehenders is their grasp of the purpose of reading. The former are more likely to understand the need to make meaning (i.e. to construct and update a situation model of the text); the latter are more likely to believe that the core purpose of reading text is the process of decoding.[1] (Some use this as an argument against teaching decoding via phonics, but the focus on early decoding is (a) balanced by the aspects of reading instruction, and (b) necessary for many if later comprehension is to be facilitated.) The act of expecting a text to make sense in some form is sometimes called 'setting a **standard of coherence'**.[2] As well as setting a generally lower standard of coherence, poor comprehenders tend to be less flexible in matching this standard to the purpose of reading. In contrast, a good comprehender will change their standard of coherence depending on whether they are reading for pleasure, searching for information, preparing to be asked questions, etc.[3] This flexible use of **comprehension monitoring** is a key component of comprehension.

Comprehension monitoring is a useful comprehension strategy that can be taught in a relatively short period of time. Research suggests that encouraging children to ask themselves questions about the text's meaning and to summarise parts of the text can lead to improvements in comprehension.[4] In addition, children can be taught to recognise when greater attention is required, for example when the vocabulary of a text is challenging or the text structure is unfamiliar. As with all comprehension strategies, this can be briefly explained and modelled before scaffolding is provided to support children's use of the strategy independently when required.[5] This helps children to see reading as something akin to a problem-solving task and to appreciate that the ongoing construction of meaning from text is the ultimate purpose of reading, something that requires their conscious attention. (See Chapter 21 for more on the practicalities of teaching comprehension monitoring.)

As discussed in Chapter 7, some contrast the brief use of comprehension strategies with a content-focused approach to reading.[6] Beck and McKeown (2002) described a content-focused method of supporting children's comprehension called 'Questioning the Author' in which the questions asked of children (described as 'queries') focus on the author's intent and success in communicating meaning.[7] For example, children might be asked, 'What is the author trying to say?' or 'What has the author tried to communicate so far?' This ensures children understand that writing and reading involves direct communication between a writer and their audience, and that the ideas communicated might not be clear or complete. Referring to the author behind the writing is a powerful way to understand a text, even when (or especially when) the author has intentionally written in an impersonal style (e.g. in a newspaper article). Nevertheless, this view of teaching reading does not necessarily clash with the teaching of comprehension strategies. Asking children to visualise what the author is communicating in some way or to summarise what the author has communicated in a given paragraph is an approach that develops comprehension monitoring *and* ensures that children engage with the content of the text in a productive fashion. The potential ways that such teaching can be employed is discussed in more depth in Chapter 21.

─────────────── In a nutshell … ───────────────

- Model the process of monitoring comprehension when a text is more challenging in some way, including the re-reading of sentences or paragraphs where required for understanding.
- Briefly teach children to self-question (including summarising and visualising) and then encourage independent use of this comprehension strategy in children's reading practice; ensure that this is always undertaken in relation to reading content.
- Ensure that the teaching of this comprehension strategy is embedded in the ultimate purpose of reading – deriving meaning from texts chosen for their content.

Other implications for the classroom

One of the key aspects of effective teaching is avoiding the 'curse of knowledge' in which experts find it difficult to imagine the incomprehension of novice learners and to make appropriate allowances.[8] Comprehension monitoring, another aspect of reading that can be described as metacognitive (see Chapter 7), requires teachers to recognise something that seems so obvious to us, that the fundamental purpose of reading is to gain understanding. Children need to be shown repeatedly the processes involved with monitoring comprehension. Teachers must model checking for understanding at the end of a paragraph, re-reading sentences that are difficult to unpick and working out what they think an author meant by a given word or phrase. This may even mean that teachers need to manufacture situations where they can pretend to be confused by a text so that they can model the process of dealing with that confusion by slowing down and re-reading sentences or entire paragraphs. Equally, teachers may model their own curiosity at a part of a text that seems to remain beyond explanation, showing the class that they will keep this in mind as they read further, expecting that the text will reveal the relevant information in due course. Teachers must help children develop their own sense of the delicate balance required to know when to re-read to avoid confusion and when to accept that the relevant information will become apparent with further reading. Through thinking aloud, teachers can show children exactly what reading is all about and the level of self-awareness required to comprehend well.

---------------- Questions for professional discussions ----------------

- How might comprehension monitoring differ between text types (e.g. between mystery stories and information texts)?
- Does the teaching of other subjects have something equivalent to the modelling of comprehension monitoring in reading instruction? What are the differences and similarities between these metacognitive processes?

---------------- Retrieval quiz ----------------

1   What is meant by 'standard of coherence'?
2   Those who struggle with comprehension are less likely to match their standard of coherence to their purpose for reading. What might this look like in practice?
3   To aid their comprehension monitoring, children can be taught to self-question. How else can they be encouraged to monitor their own comprehension?

Further reading

- Oakhill, J., Cain, K. and Elbro, C. (2014). *Understanding and Teaching Reading Comprehension: A Handbook*. London: Routledge.

References

1   Oakhill, J., Cain, K. and Elbro, C. (2014). *Understanding and Teaching Reading Comprehension: A Handbook*. London: Routledge; Cain, K. (1999). Ways of reading: How knowledge and use of strategies are related to reading comprehension. *British Journal of Developmental Psychology*, 17(2), 293–309; Yuill, N. M. and Oakhill, J. V. (1991). *Children's Problems in Text Comprehension: An Experimental Investigation*. Cambridge: Cambridge University Press.

2   Oakhill, Cain and Elbro (2014); Perfetti, C. A., Landi, N. and Oakhill, J. (2005). The acquisition of reading comprehension skill. In Snowling, M. J. and Hulme, C. (eds), *The Science of Reading: A Handbook* (Blackwell Handbooks of Developmental Psychology). Oxford: Blackwell Publishing, 227–247.

3   Oakhill, J. V., Hartt, J. and Samols, D. (2005). Levels of comprehension monitoring and working memory in good and poor comprehenders. *Reading and Writing*, 18, 657–686; Kaakinen, J. and Hyönä, J. (2010). Task effects on eye movements during reading. *Journal of Experimental Psychology: Learning, Memory, and Cognition*, 36, 1561–1566; Connor, C., Radach, R., Vorstius, C., Day, S. L., McLean, L. and Morrison, F. J. (2015). Individual differences in fifth graders' reading and language predict their comprehension monitoring development: An eye-movement study. *Scientific Studies of Reading: The Official Journal of the Society for the Scientific Study of Reading*, 19, 114–134.

4   Oakhill, Cain and Elbro (2014).

5   de Sousa, I. and Oakhill, J. (1996). Do levels of interest have an effect on children's comprehension monitoring performance?. *British Journal of Educational Psychology*, 66(4), 471–482; Brown, A. L., Palincsar, A. S. and Armbruster, B. B. (1984). Instructing comprehension-fostering activities in interactive learning situations. In Mandl, H., Stein, N. L. and Trabasso, T. (eds), *Learning and Comprehension of Text*. Hillsdale, NJ: Erlbuam, 255–286.

6   McKeown, M. G., Beck, I. L. and Blake, R. G. (2009). Rethinking reading comprehension instruction: A comparison of instruction for strategies and content approaches. *Reading Research Quarterly*, 44(3), 218–253.

7   Beck, I. L. and McKeown, M. G. (2002). Questioning the author: Making sense of social studies. *Educational Leadership*, 59(3), 44–47.

8   Heath, C. and Heath, D. (2006). The curse of knowledge. *Harvard Business Review*, 84(12), 20–23; Newton, E. L. (1991). The rocky road from actions to intentions. Unpublished PhD dissertation. Stanford University.

9

INFERENCE

Types of inference

Inference in reading is the use of present information alongside reasoning to work out something that is not otherwise clearly stated. The ability to infer is necessary for reading as there is inevitably information within any text which is shared with a reader implicitly rather than explicitly. Take this group of sentences:

> *Grasping his CV, Diego looked through the window at the growing puddles and searched for his umbrella. It was only after a minute of ransacking his house that he remembered that he had lent it to his sister. There was no other option; he would have to go by car.*

There are many inferences that we must make to construct a useful situation model for Diego's actions and motives. Here are just a few:

1   Diego's 'CV' suggests that he is on his way to an important event relating to employment, perhaps a job interview.
2   The 'growing puddles' show that it is raining.
3   Diego does not wish to get wet.
4   'he' refers to Diego.
5   'it' refers to the umbrella.
6   Diego's sister has not returned his umbrella.
7   Going by car is an alternative means of travel that will keep Diego dry.

As we can see, inference relies on our knowledge of the vocabulary and syntax of a text, our worldly knowledge relating to the context and our understanding of text structure (in this case, narrative). The inferences that we make in the process of understanding a text can be divided into two types: **local cohesion inferences** and **global coherence inferences**.

Local cohesion inferences, sometimes known as text-connecting inference, are those which directly connect elements within a text, often using single words or phrases.[1] These come in different forms:

- pronouns (e.g. 'he', 'it', 'they')
- nouns preceded by the definite article (e.g. '*the* cat' after having introduced '*a* cat')
- connectives (e.g. 'previously', 'while', 'instead', 'because')
- missing words (e.g. 'He jumped in the river and his brother *did too*.')
- nouns referred to in a different way (e.g. 'He peered into *the cavern*. The *dark expanse* echoed.').

In the text about Diego above, inference (4) is an example of local cohesion inference. Without local cohesion inferences the sentences of the text don't fit together to make an integrated whole.

In contrast, global coherence inferences, sometimes known as gap-filling inference, are those which rely on general knowledge or wider vocabulary to fill a gap that has been left by the writer. They might support us to understand the setting, character motivations, themes or purpose of a text. Inference (1) is an example of a global coherence inference. While global coherence inferences aren't necessary to see how sentences fit together, without them the text's meaning seems vague and the wider elements of the text – plot, themes, purpose, etc. – are impossible to grasp.

Inferences can also be defined as either necessary or elaborative. **Necessary inferences**, as the name suggests, are those that are necessary for full appreciation of meaning. In fact, all of the inferences (1) – (7) are necessary inferences. (All local cohesion inferences are necessary, by definition, but only some global coherence inferences are necessary.) **Elaborative inferences** are those that go beyond that which is required to understand the meaning of the text. For example, we might assume that there is a reason that Diego was keen to not use his car; it might be unreliable, or he might expect a traffic jam. Such elaborative inferences can be useful, but just as often they are a hindrance to understanding and need to be supressed to some extent. In short, both necessary local cohesion inferences and necessary global coherence inferences are critical in the constructing and updating of a situation model for adequate comprehension of a text. So what? Why is it worth knowing about these types of inference? Crucially, it allows teachers to appreciate the range of inferences that a child might be struggling to make, and thus to consider in advance what elements of a text might require discussion.

Is inference a skill?

In the statutory, end-of-primary-school reading assessments in England, questions that apparently seek to measure the skill of inference account for around 40 per cent of the marks given out to students.[2] You would be forgiven for presuming then that inference is a transferable skill that can be taught directly. There is no evidence base whatsoever to support this view and mere thoughtful reflection also reveals it not to be the case: give a child words that they understand well (and can decode fluently) in uncomplicated sentence structures in a familiar context and they will infer plenty of meaning. Equally, give a well-read adult a text containing words that they don't understand in complicated sentence structures and an unfamiliar context and they will infer next to nothing. Each inference relates to a specific bit of text and is the result of knowledge: knowledge of words and syntax, knowledge of the world and knowledge of text structures. Thus, a person's ability to infer meaning from a text – much like language comprehension in total – is built up like the adding of dots to a pointillist painting. In the case of language comprehension, the dots are fragments of knowledge about words, about the world and about text structures. While each dot may seem discrete as it is added by the teacher and student acting in concert, it gains its meaning from its connections and context. As teachers of inference – and language comprehension more broadly – the best we can do is to spread the dots evenly across the canvas and dedicate time to giving each student a rich, full canvas from which to make meaning.

What does this mean in practice? It means engaging children in lots of worthwhile texts; it means discussing vocabulary, particularly the pronouns and connectives of local cohesion inferences;[3] it means picking apart sentence structures using close reading;[4] it means analysing various text structures, including the use of graphic organisers;[5] and it means teaching a curriculum that systematically and thoughtfully increases children's understanding of the world. All of this will be discussed in the coming chapters.

Is that it? Is there nothing else that can be done to support children's ability to make inferences other than the meticulous, well-planned development of their knowledge of words, of the world and of text structures? Not quite. While inference is certainly not a generic, transferable skill, it is true that children sometimes fail to make inferences even when they have the requisite knowledge.[6] There is evidence to suggest that the comprehension strategy discussed in the previous chapter – comprehension monitoring via self-questioning (including summarising and visualising) – applies equally to situations where children need to make inferences.[7] Teaching children about the *need* to make inferences is an essential component of comprehension monitoring and one that supports children's understanding of text.[8]

———————————————— In a nutshell … ————————

- Know that there are two types of inferences necessary to discern the meaning of a text: local cohesion (text-connecting) inferences and global coherence (gap-filling) inferences.
- Know that global coherence inferences can also be elaborative (i.e. go beyond the text) and that elaborative inferences can inhibit understanding; consider limiting the elaborative inferences you discuss with children, particularly if they may be struggling to comprehend the text's meaning.

- Avoid teaching inference as a generic skill; when children learn to make an inference in a given situation, they have learned the bit of knowledge or vocabulary that has allowed that inference; they have *not* developed some underlying inference ability.
- Improve children's inferences by teaching a broad, carefully planned curriculum; by teaching and discussing vocabulary (especially pronouns and connectives); and by teaching children about different text structures.
- Teach the need to make inferences, sometimes with a little deliberation required, as part of comprehension monitoring.

Other implications for the classroom

Education is an exceptionally complicated business. It can be tempting to cling on to methods of teaching that are based on comforting simplifications of complex processes. School leaders – pressured by the need to improve assessment data – can be forgiven for preferring the simplistic concept of inference as generic skill to the multifaceted reality. After all, this view provides a shortcut to success: *get the children doing lots of inference questions in preparation for the assessments, and that will do the trick.* Nevertheless, inference – and reading comprehension more generally – simply doesn't work like this. School leaders must rid themselves of the 'quick fix' mentality that sees countless hours thrown at ineffective practices. Children's ability to infer relies on their grasp of words, phrases and syntax; their appreciation of different text structures; and their knowledge of the world, all of which are the result of their entire education – at school and at home. No amount of misguided inference skill lessons will make this untrue.

Thankfully, the alternative to children churning in vain through countless inference questions is one that all teachers should relish. Teaching reading in a way that is more aligned with research would see more time spent appreciating stories, more time unpicking the intricacies of language choices and more time learning about the world through fascinating information texts. Leaving behind the simplistic view of inference and reading comprehension empowers schools to take on the daunting but exhilarating task of selecting valuable texts and then getting children to interact with them in a way that will open their minds and broaden their horizons.

——————— Questions for professional discussions ———————

- To what extent has the view of inference as a generic skill been present in the schools in which you have worked? What consequences did this have on the teaching of reading?
- In what circumstances might it be worthwhile to support children to make elaborative inferences? When might this be counterproductive?

───────────────── Retrieval quiz ─────────────────

1   What is the difference between local cohesion inferences and global coherence inferences?
2   What is the difference between necessary inferences and elaborative inferences?
3   How does children's learning across the entirety of the curriculum impact their ability to make inferences?

Further reading

- Oakhill, J., Cain, K. and Elbro, C. (2014). *Understanding and Teaching Reading Comprehension: A Handbook*. London: Routledge.

References

1   Cain, K. and Oakhill, J. (2014). Reading comprehension and vocabulary: Is vocabulary more important for some aspects of comprehension? *L'Annee Psychologique*, 114(4), 647–662.
2   *Perverse Incentives: The KS2 Reading SAT and the Myth of Generic Reading Comprehension Skills*. Teachwell, 23 May. Available at: www.teach-well.com/perverse-incentives-the-ks2-reading-sat-and-the-myth-of-generic-reading-comprehension-skills/ (accessed 30 November 2020).
3   Geva, E. and Ryan, E. B. (1985). Use of conjunctions in expository texts by skilled and less skilled readers. *Journal of Reading Behavior*, 17(4), 331–346.
4   Oakhill, J., Cain, K. and Elbro, C. (2014). *Understanding and Teaching Reading Comprehension: A Handbook*. London: Routledge.
5   National Reading Panel (US), National Institute of Child Health, Human Development (US), National Reading Excellence Initiative, National Institute for Literacy (US), United States. Public Health Service, & United States Department of Health (2000). *Report of the National Reading Panel: Teaching children to read: An evidence-based assessment of the scientific research literature on reading and its implications for reading instruction: Reports of the subgroups*. National Institute of Child Health and Human Development, National Institutes of Health; Gallini, J., Spires, H., Terry, S. and Gleaton, J. (1993). The influence of macro and micro-level cognitive strategies training on text learning. *Journal of Research and Development in Education*, 26(3), 164–178.
6   Oakhill, Cain and Elbro (2014).
7   Francey, G. and Cain, K. (2015). Effect of imagery training on children's comprehension of pronouns. *The Journal of Educational Research*, 108(1), 1–9.
8   Ibid.

10

TEXT STRUCTURE

Although spoken language sometimes conforms to particular structures (e.g. political speeches, academic lectures, etc.), it is most commonly experienced in a relatively unstructured form due to the improvised nature of conversations. In contrast, most written text is planned in advance and conforms to specific structures that exist to support the establishment of meaning. (Social media provides something of an exception to this, though one can argue that these too have limits and informal rules by which people tend to abide.)

Written texts can be broadly divided into two categories: literature (fictional narratives, poetry and drama) and informational texts (which can have narrative or expository structures) (Figure 10.1).

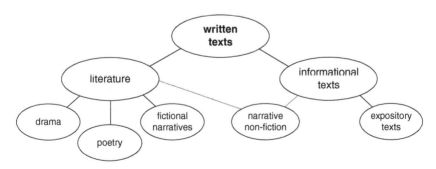

Figure 10.1   Written texts divided into two categories

Within each category there are particular genres, the understanding of which supports a reader's ability to extract meaning.[1] A knowledge of the typical structure of these genres helps readers to form accurate expectations, to search through a text for given information and to understand how different parts of a text link together.[2] Thus, teaching children about the structure of different genres of text (and the structures of literature and informational texts more generally) can support children's comprehension.[3]

Literature

Through the experience and discussion of dramatic texts (i.e. play scripts), poetry and narratives, children can be taught both implicitly and explicitly about the typical structure of these texts. (Note that, as the diagram above shows, non-fiction narrative texts such as biographies can be considered as both literature and as informational texts.)[4] For example, having learned that fictional narratives tend to contain central characters seeking to achieve a goal, children are more likely as they read to give particular attention to the motivations of characters or the obstacles they face, helping the children to construct and update a situation model. Equally, understanding the concept of a beginning, middle and end – with conflict, rising stakes and a denouement – can support children's comprehension (not to mention their ability to write stories themselves). Dramatic texts, poetry and narratives can, of course, also be sub-categorised into different genres. Knowing the features of different genres (e.g. fairy tales, creation myths, mystery stories, etc.) can also be useful, though children need to be made aware that there is overlap between genres and that authors can intentionally subvert the expectations of a given genre for effect.

Informational texts

Informational texts constitute an increasing proportion of classroom reading material as children progress through school.[5] Just as with literature, there are different types and genres of informational text (e.g. essays, speeches, journalistic articles). Beyond the discussion of genre, there are further ways of considering the underlying structures of informational texts that children can be beneficially taught.[6] Oakhill Cain and Elbro (2014) described five different underlying structures for informational texts: description; sequence; compare and contrast; cause and effect; and problem and solution.[7] These are often combined within single texts. Considering these different structures of informational texts can help children to perceive the necessary inferences that they need to make, something that is especially important given that informational texts often contain unfamiliar concepts and vocabulary.

Graphic organisers

Different text structures can be related to different graphic organisers to support children's understanding.[8] For example, the points within a compare and contrast informational text may be represented using a Venn diagram or a 'double spray' diagram (Figure 10.2).

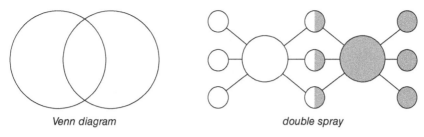

Venn diagram   *double spray*

Figure 10.2   Venn diagram and double spray diagram

Graphic organisers, such as flow diagrams, are equally suited to the description of literature text types and are an excellent way to visualise text structure and support children's understanding.[9] Using these, and teaching other aspects of text structure, can be undertaken as an integrated part of reading sessions, supported by discussion and questioning. Such teaching can also take place in writing sessions and across the curriculum, whenever a text in its entirety needs to be summarised and understood.

─────────────────── In a nutshell … ───────────────────

- Understand and teach the structures and typical features of different types of text.
- Ensure children understand that different text types can be combined or even subverted intentionally by writers.
- Consider the use of graphic organisers to help children to visualise different text structures.

Other implications for the classroom

Children can and should be exposed to a wide variety of reading material in reading lessons. It would represent a missed opportunity, however, if we only considered text structure in the context of reading lessons. While learning to write, children should analyse a variety of texts to grasp their typical languages features and structure. Equally, this analysis of relevant texts can be integrated into lessons across the curriculum, be it the study of diaries as sources in history lessons or expository texts in a science lessons.

In my experience, children's learning of a given text structure often equates to the study of one example at a time, usually a model text written by the teacher or found online. The purpose of this is that children are expected to imbibe the essence of the text, ready to create a version of their own. The challenge here – one that children struggle to meet – involves finding the perfect balance needed to alter the model text just the right amount: too much innovation and the child's version won't fulfil the teacher's list of success criteria; too little innovation and the child's version is little more than a copy of the model text with a few words changed. The remedy to this is the use of multiple models. If a child is to be able to understand the structure of a newspaper article to an extent that allows them to create one that deviates significantly from a model text, they must see several newspaper articles, preferably ones that show the variety of this text type. Ideally, they would also see contrasting non-examples, texts that have many of the same features as a newspaper article but that lack the essential ingredients. Bluntly, if children are to understand a text type, they must see a wide variety of examples and non-examples. This will support their writing as much as it develops their reading.

──────────── Questions for professional discussions ────────────

- What would be the advantages of creating a graphic organiser to represent a text in the lesson as children watched? What would be the advantages of preparing it in advance?
- Is there a trade-off between analysis of certain texts, specifically stories and poetry, and the appreciation of them, or can analysis and appreciation be mutually reinforcing? If the latter, what might be done to emphasise this?

──────────── Retrieval quiz ────────────

1 Into what two broad categories can written texts be divided?
2 How might a graphic organiser be used to support a child's understanding of a story? How might this differ from a graphic organiser used to support their understanding of an expository text?

Further reading

- Caviglioli, O. (2019). *Dual Coding with Teachers*. Woodbridge: John Catt.
- Oakhill, J., Cain, K. and Elbro, C. (2014). *Understanding and Teaching Reading Comprehension: A Handbook*. London: Routledge.

References

1   Zwaan, R. A. (1994). Effect of genre expectations on text comprehension. *Journal of Experimental Psychology: Learning, Memory, and Cognition*, 20(4), 920–933.
2   Oakhill, J., Cain, K. and Elbro, C. (2019). Reading comprehension and reading comprehension difficulties. In Kilpatrick, D. A., Joshi, R. M. and Wagner, R. K. (eds), *Reading Development and Difficulties*. Cham: Springer, 83–115.
3   Paris, A. H. and Paris, S. G. (2007). Teaching narrative comprehension strategies to first graders. *Cognition and Instruction*, 25(1), 1–44.
4   Association for Supervision and Curriculum Development (2012). *Text Genres*. Available at: www.ascd.org/ASCD/pdf/siteASCD/publications/ascdexpress/7.21grades6-12-fig1.PDF (accessed 30 November 2020).
5   Venezky, R. L. (2000). The origins of the present-day chasm between adult literacy needs and school literacy instruction. *Scientific Studies of Reading*, 4(1), 19–39.
6   Meyer, B. J. and Freedle, R. O. (1984). Effects of discourse type on recall. *American Educational Research Journal*, 21(1), 121–143.
7   Oakhill, J., Cain, K. and Elbro, C. (2014). *Understanding and Teaching Reading Comprehension: A Handbook*. London: Routledge.
8   National Reading Panel (US), National Institute of Child Health, Human Development (US), National Reading Excellence Initiative, National Institute for Literacy (US), United States. Public Health Service, & United States Department of Health (2000). *Report of the National Reading Panel: Teaching children to read: An evidence-based assessment of the scientific research literature on reading and its implications for reading instruction: Reports of the subgroups*. National Institute of Child Health and Human Development, National Institutes of Health.
9   Ibid.; Corbett, P. and Strong, J. (2011). *Talk for Writing Across the Curriculum: How to Teach Non-Fiction Writing 5–12 Years*. Maidenhead: McGraw-Hill Education; Caviglioli, O. (2019). *Dual Coding with Teachers*. Woodbridge: John Catt.

11

VOCABULARY

Unsurprisingly, there is a well-established association between the extent of a child's vocabulary and their language comprehension abilities.[1] A useful lens through which to view vocabulary and its acquisition is that of **vocabulary breadth** and **vocabulary depth**.[2] The breadth of a person's vocabulary is simply the number of words that they can recognise, at least to some extent. (Vocabulary that can be understood *and* used is called one's active vocabulary; that which is *only* understood is called one's passive vocabulary. In the case of reading, it is the span of one's passive vocabulary that matters most.) The depth of a person's vocabulary is the extent to which the many facets of words are known and the ways in which words are connected to a wide variety of contexts. Take the word 'steal'. A young child may only understand this word in terms of the physical act of taking something without permission. Most adults, however, will understand the word in various other contexts and phrases. Their rich network of understanding will allow them to understand that one can 'steal an election', 'steal a heart' and 'steal a march'; they will know that no crime has been committed when someone proudly declares that their new shoes were 'a steal at this price'. In short, most adults' understanding of the word 'steal' has considerable depth as the word is for them part of a rich network of meaning. Vocabulary breadth and depth are both important to reading in different ways.

Imagine a child trying to decode the word 'throw' for the very first time. Thanks to their knowledge of various sound–spelling correspondences learned through phonics, they will likely be confident in determining the sounds represented by the <th> and <r> graphemes in this word. But what about <ow>? Having learned over time that this spelling can represent different phonemes, the child has a decision to make: does this new word that they are decoding end with a sound that rhymes with 'how'? Or does this new word end with a sound that rhymes with 'mow'? It is the breadth of their vocabulary that comes to the rescue. Using phoneme manipulation skills, the child rapidly tries out both possibilities and quickly realises that they already have a word in their vocabulary that matches one of those sounds. They have matched the spelling of the word 'throw' to the pronunciation stored in their mind and begun orthographically mapping the word. A few more acts of decoding like this (or fewer) and they will add 'throw' to their ever-expanding list of sight words (or words that they can process *as if* by sight). This process of orthographic mapping is dependent on a reader's vocabulary. If the spellings of words cannot be matched to a stored pronunciation, then orthographic mapping cannot occur. When it comes to decoding, in most cases it is vocabulary breadth that matters …

… But not always. Imagine the same child is decoding the word 'great' in the sentence, 'We had a great time.' They are confident in their decoding of the <g>, <r> and <t> graphemes, but unsure at first whether the <ea> grapheme represents an /ee/ phoneme or an /ay/ phoneme. Manipulating the possible phonemes, they recognise that both options sound like words they recognise in their vocabulary: 'great' and 'greet'. The child's vocabulary breadth has got them this far, but it is now the depth of their vocabulary that becomes crucial. Using the context of the sentence, they see that the word must be 'great'. (While they are perhaps not yet aware of the formal names for word classes, the idea that 'great' often acts as an adjective is already an inherent part of their vocabulary depth.) In this case, both vocabulary breadth and depth were essential to the accurate decoding of this word. Nevertheless, vocabulary breadth tends to matter a lot more for decoding while vocabulary depth has the greater impact on comprehension.[3] Naturally, just recognising a word isn't enough to support the derivation of meaning from a text, and it is estimated that around 90 per cent of words in a given text need to be understood *to an appropriate depth* to allow for any comprehension to take place.[4] Willingham (2017) went further, suggesting that 98 per cent of words need to be understood for what he termed 'comfortable comprehension'.[5]

As is the case with language comprehension generally, the relative importance of vocabulary knowledge to reading comprehension increases as children progress through primary school. The link between vocabulary and reading development is all the more profound due to what Stanovich (2009) labelled 'the Matthew effect', a name for the reciprocal relationship between word-knowledge and comprehension: a virtuous cycle in which children with greater vocabulary breadth and depth decode more and understand more of what they read, which leads them to expand their vocabulary more efficiently.[6] (Even though good readers can only deduce around 15 per cent of the unknown words they encounter, over time this still adds up to a substantial gain.)[7] This reinforcing cycle just emphasises how important it is to ensure that vocabulary is taught effectively.

So, how can this be done? It certainly isn't the case that teachers can hope to directly teach most of the words that children need to learn.[8] The vast majority of words that children learn are not directly taught, and trying to explicitly and thoroughly teach, say, an extra 1,000 words per year would likely take too much curriculum time to be viable. (For perspective, the average child adds around 3,000 words per year to their vocabulary.)[9] Nevertheless, ensuring that children are undertaking lots of reading inside school (and outside school as well, where possible) is the first step in supporting vocabulary development.[10]

How else can we support vocabulary development? As Seidenberg (2017) asserted, 'learning vocabulary is a Big Data problem solved with a small amount of timely instruction and a lot of statistical learning' (p. 111).[11] Lots of reading and a language-rich learning environment take care of the 'statistical learning' (i.e. that which children undertake via implicit pattern spotting). Despite the relative dearth of evidence on the effective teaching of vocabulary, there are three sensible ways to tackle Seidenberg's 'small amount of timely instruction':

1   Select and then teach particularly useful words.
2   Teach children some of the essential etymology and morphology of the English language so that they can more easily discern word meanings for themselves.
3   Teach unfamiliar words at the moment that they are encountered in texts.

The most useful words: tier two vocabulary

Time is the teacher's most precious commodity. There is only so much time available to teach vocabulary, so deciding on what words are most worth teaching is key. Beck, McKeown and Kucan (2013) suggest a sensible way to do this is by assigning words to one of three tiers:[12]

> **Tier one words** are those that children will very likely encounter and learn in their daily lives (e.g. 'table', 'jump', 'through', 'because').
>
> **Tier two words** are those that children will not commonly encounter in their daily lives, but they are also not specific to given subjects. They are useful across many subjects, but often end up overlooked precisely because they are not associated with one academic discipline in particular (e.g. 'emerged', 'precise', 'society', 'whereas').
>
> **Tier three words** are those that are specific to individual subjects. These tend to be taught within specific subject areas out of necessity (e.g. 'radius', 'octave', 'pointillism', 'alkali').

Teaching *tier two* words is a sensible way to equip children with precisely the words that they are less likely to learn but are still likely to encounter, particularly as they progress through school.

But which tier two words should be selected? There is no one right way to answer this question. However, I will talk you through how I selected a list of 345 tier two words to be taught to children between the ages of 7 and 11 years old. Through this, I hope you will understand the process by which such a selection can be made.

Coxhead's (2000) academic word list was created by finding words that appeared repeatedly and commonly across academic literature.[13] The 570 words contained in the academic word list account for roughly 10 per cent of all words used in academic texts. The list was created with the explicit aim of supporting people before entry into tertiary education, so some of the words are unsuitable for primary education. Using experience gained from teaching primary-age children for over a decade, I selected the words on the list that I deemed suitable for children between the ages of 7 and 11 years old and that fitted the definition of tier two vocabulary. However, the academic word list automatically discounts the 2,000 most common words in written English, many of which would count as tier two vocabulary for children aged 7–11. To counter this, I also selected tier two vocabulary from available lists of the most common words in spoken and written English.[14] Naturally, the final list is the result of personal judgement; there are sensible arguments for the exclusion of some words on the list and inclusion of some words that are not. Regardless, the full list of 345 words (something I imaginatively titled 'the 345 list') can be found in Appendix A at the end of this book, along with a suggested timetable for introducing and revising these words with children based on their perceived difficulty (Appendix C). While a discrete approach to vocabulary such as this can be effective on its own, ideally the vast majority of tier two vocabulary that is most important for children to learn should be integrated into the wider curriculum so that it is also taught and grasped in context. If this integration is completed, the order in which the vocabulary is explicitly taught can be synchronised with the wider curriculum. In this way, discrete vocabulary lessons can provide an opportunity for retrieval and broader application of the words that have been introduced in science, history, geography, etc.

Morphology

Earlier in this book, you will have read – and no doubt understood – the word 'comprehender'. Although it is a word directly taken from an academic text, as I sit here typing, a squiggly red line is telling me that 'comprehender' doesn't exist as a 'real' word (according to *my* laptop, at least). A quick glance at a dictionary confirms that this word is, at best, pretty rare. It may well be the first time you've ever seen it written down. (It is, after all, a bit *clunky*.) And yet, I have no doubt that you understood it to mean 'one who comprehends'. You knew this because you have either been taught, or learned independently, about **morphology**. In the context of language, morphology refers to the structure of words and their parts. In the case of 'comprehender', you immediately recognised that the '-er' part of the word meant that a noun was being made from a verb, as in the words 'walk<u>er</u>', 'bit<u>er</u>' and 'fight<u>er</u>'. (Note that '-er' can, among other functions, also turn an adjective into a comparative adjective, e.g. 'fast<u>er</u>'.) These parts of words are called **morphemes**. Morphemes are the smallest units of meaning in a language. For example, 'conceal' has one morpheme, the meaning of which is 'hide'.

In comparison, 'concea<u>led</u>' has two morphemes; the '-ed' morpheme signals the past tense, as it regularly does in English. There are three morphemes in '<u>un</u>concea<u>led</u>'. The 'un-' morpheme shows negation, as it does in words like '<u>un</u>sung', '<u>un</u>broken' and '<u>un</u>do'. In the word 'unconcealed', 'conceal' is the **root word**. Root words are the morphemes that form the base of the word and are usually central to its meaning. Through an understanding of root words and other morphemes, a language user can grasp several words after learning just one.[15] This is especially true given that more than 60 per cent of the new words that a reader encounters have a relatively transparent morphological structure and can thus be understood by breaking them down into morphemes, most of which will be familiar to the average reader.[16]

A child who has learned the word 'examine' has, if they understand common morphemes, also learned the word 'examine<u>s</u>', 'examine<u>r</u>', 'examine<u>d</u>', '<u>un</u>examined', etc. Learning to recognise morphemes helps students to decode complex words more rapidly, to learn the meanings of words and to spell them accurately.[17] This is especially vital given that around 80 per cent of words in the English language contain more than one morpheme.[18] Explicit teaching of these morphemes can support this understanding, and the timing of this explicit teaching matters.[19] Analysis of children's texts suggests that children's early reading experience consists predominantly of words with a single morpheme, so instruction in morphology is likely best reserved for later in their education.[20] I would suggest that initially children should be directed towards an understanding of the most common morphemes (e.g. -s, -ed, -ing, -er) as they encounter them naturally in reading. Later, between the ages of 7 and 11 years old, they can then be explicitly taught useful morphological patterns using words with which they are already familiar. Most of these patterns will involve **prefixes** (morphemes that add meaning at the beginning of a word) and **suffixes** (morphemes that add meaning at the end of a word). Word matrices are one way to show how these are commonly used (Figure 11.1).

		ful	ness
		s	
un	**help**	ing	
		ed	
		er	s

Figure 11.1 A word matrix for the root word 'help'

Another way is via word equations:

unmistakable → un + mistake + able

un: prefix – negative/not

mistake: root word – make an error

able: capability

Either way, the explicit teaching of morphological patterns can be undertaken as a part of classroom instruction either when introducing a new word during a lesson or as a discrete part of spelling or reading sessions.

Etymology – Latin and Greek root words

Imagine you are reading a news article when you encounter the following sentence: 'The scientists made their discovery using a new device called a subaquabioscope.' The squiggly red line is once again present on my computer screen because 'subaquabioscope' is a word I have concocted. Nonetheless, I suspect that you could hazard a decent guess about the word's meaning. If you're thinking that the device I have in mind is used for looking at living things under the surface of the water (or something along those lines) then you would be correct. But how did you know? Either consciously or unconsciously, you were using the knowledge of Latin and Greek root words that you have learned over years of using the English language. (Sub – below [Latin]; aqua – water [Latin]; bio – life [Latin/Greek]; scope – look [Greek].)

Over 60 per cent of all words in English have Latin or Greek origins;[21] this number rises to over 90 per cent for multisyllabic words and for the vocabulary of the sciences and technology.[22] For this reason, teaching children some of the most common Greek and Latin root words is potentially a way to empower them to infer meanings of unfamiliar words.[23] Teach children that the Latin root word 'tract' relates to pulling, and suddenly words like 'tractor', 'extract', 'retract', 'subtract' and 'abstract' become easier to unpick and link in ways that aid memorisation.

As with tier two vocabulary, the challenge lies in deciding which root words to choose and when to introduce them. By combining multiple lists of the most common Latin and Greek root words – and then discarding those that, according to my experience, had the least common derived words in English – I assembled a list of Latin and Greek root words that are suitable for teaching to children between the ages of 7 and 11 years old. These can be found in Appendix B at the end of the book. Appendix C suggests a timetable for teaching and revising these root words. As with tier two vocabulary, while there is a benefit to these root words being taught in a discrete fashion, ideally the majority of them should also be integrated into the wider curriculum so that they are taught and grasped in context.

Brief teaching of unfamiliar words

The teaching of vocabulary often happens spontaneously in the classroom. Children encounter an unfamiliar word in a text, and their teacher briefly explains what the word means, putting it into a few different contexts. Biemiller (2010) describes this teaching as the use of 'drop-in words', a method claimed to be particularly effective for concrete words (e.g. 'skylight', 'tentacle', 'crepuscular') and words that have synonyms already familiar to children (e.g. 'pursuit', 'despair', 'crave').[24] As long as this doesn't overly disrupt the flow of reading a text, this practice is a great way to supplement the systematic vocabulary teaching described above.

Vocabulary teaching techniques

As discussed, vocabulary instruction should include in-the-moment teaching as children encounter unfamiliar words in texts, the explicit teaching of particularly valuable (tier two) words and the teaching of morphology and root words to support children's ability to independently derive word meanings. But what about teaching techniques? Effective vocabulary instruction tends to have four characteristics:[25]

1 A child-friendly definition is given.
2 The word is contextualised in sentences, including non-examples where necessary.
3 Children are exposed to the word multiple times.
4 Children actively use the word, either in speech or writing.

Let's see what this may look like in practice. Imagine a teacher wishes to introduce children to the word 'announce'. First she might say the following:

> The word 'announce' is a verb that means to 'state something clearly'. It is used when we feel we are saying something important that we think people need to hear. I probably wouldn't 'announce' to my friends that I was having jam sandwiches for lunch; I would just tell them that. However, I might 'announce' that I was having a birthday party or that I had made an important decision.

If this were just some in-the-moment teaching, then the word might be noted down for later retrieval and the lesson would continue. However, if this were a discrete (but brief) vocabulary lesson, then the children might then be asked to use the word in context: 'Say this sentence starter to your partner and then finish it: "The firefighter announced that …"'. In this way, the class have had the word defined and contextualised in a child-friendly way, and they have had the chance to think about the word's meaning by using it. Along with subsequent purposeful retrieval, which is a key aspect of all teaching, such vocabulary instruction increases the chances that children will add the word into their vocabulary, adding another dot to their pointillist canvas of reading comprehension.

―――――――――――――――――――――― In a nutshell … ――――――――――――――――

- Appreciate the importance of vocabulary breadth and depth.
- Ensure that children are encountering and decoding large volumes of text in reading sessions and across the rest of the curriculum.
- Maximise the value of in-the-moment vocabulary teaching by defining and contextualising unfamiliar words in child-friendly ways and, where time allows, asking them to use the word.
- Consider teaching carefully chosen tier two vocabulary and Latin and Greek root words.
- Support children's understanding of morphology through explicit teaching of common prefixes and suffixes.

Other implications for the classroom

While this chapter has focused on the more structured aspects of vocabulary instruction, each day teachers provide a language-rich environment that supports children's development of word knowledge. Much of teaching involves a subtle balancing act that takes years to master between too much challenge and too little, and this is no less true when it comes to vocabulary choice. As teachers, we naturally adapt the language we use to find the balance between being understood and challenging children by exposing them to new words. I would argue that a simple heuristic can allow us to get the best of both worlds: when explaining something that is new to children, err on the side of comprehensibility. Use relatively simple sentence structures and words with which we are confident the children are familiar. However, the rest of the time, be bold in your vocabulary choices, explaining new words where possible, but also accepting that the occasional lack of comprehension will be a worthwhile trade-off for children being exposed to a broad vocabulary in a real context.

Until recently, my conscious grasp of Latin and Greek root words was borderline non-existent. Learning about root words like 'lev' (relating to 'lift', e.g. 'elevate', 'levity' and 'leverage') and 'dyna' (relating to power, e.g. 'dynamic', 'dynamite' and 'dynasty') has proven to be enlightening and useful. I would argue that in terms of effort to payoff ratio, there is no one thing a person can do to boost their understanding of language (and of their world) that is as effective as memorising 100 or so Latin and Greek root words. Once learned, they offer a key to the parts of language that are otherwise most mystifying. Such knowledge will greatly support your teaching, and you will find yourself sharing it enthusiastically with children, recognising that they are entitled to grasp one of the keys to unlocking the English language. However, I would recommend the learning of Latin and Greek root words not just to teachers, but to anyone who wants to feel more at home in the English language and more able to grasp its patterns.

Reading and writing are inherently linked, so please forgive a brief diversion into the subject of teaching writing. The teaching of vocabulary in primary school writing lessons is, in my experience, often done in a way that is unintentionally detrimental to children's ability to use the language. I have regularly observed teachers extolling the virtues of 'powerful vocabulary' or 'impressive vocabulary' at the expense of words that are deemed not fit for any purpose. Often these banned words are some of the most exceptionally useful ones in our language, such as 'said' and 'good'. I understand the motivations behind such teaching. We want children to explore new vocabulary, and banning certain words or discussing how 'delectable' might be a more interesting choice than 'tasty' can seem like a simple way to nudge children to achieve this. The problem is that this gives children a false impression about the aims of writing and the value of a broad, deep vocabulary. The only reason to choose one word over another is because it more effectively communicates meaning. We should seek precision in our vocabulary choices, preferring a rarer word only when it communicates meaning that would not be contained within a more common word. Whether vocabulary is 'powerful' or 'impressive' should not be a consideration for any writer, and certainly not one that we communicate to children, consciously or otherwise.

Questions for professional discussions

- Considering the tier two vocabulary contained in Appendix A and the Latin and Greek root words contained in Appendix B, where might these words be embedded into subjects across the curriculum in your school(s)?
- When reading aloud to children, what might be the advantages of pausing regularly to explain unfamiliar vocabulary? In contrast, what might be the advantages of making a note of unfamiliar vocabulary and explaining the meanings of the words later on? When might it be advisable to simply read the unfamiliar word and move on?

Retrieval quiz

1. What is the difference between vocabulary breadth and depth?
2. In what way is there a reciprocal relationship between vocabulary breadth and decoding?
3. What are the criteria that define a 'tier two' word?
4. How can an understanding of morphology support children to understand the meaning of an unfamiliar word?
5. What are the four characteristics that tend to be part of effective vocabulary instruction?

Further reading

- Beck, I. L., McKeown, M. G. and Kucan, L. (2013). *Bringing Words to Life: Robust Vocabulary Instruction*. New York: Guilford Press.
- Quigley, A. (2018). *Closing the Vocabulary Gap*. Abingdon: Routledge.

References

1 McKeown, M. G., Beck, I. L., Omanson, R. C. and Perfetti, C. A. (1983). The effects of long-term vocabulary instruction on reading comprehension: A replication. *Journal of Reading Behavior*, 15(1), 3–18; Ouellette, G. P. (2006). What's meaning got to do with it: The role of vocabulary in word reading and reading comprehension. *Journal of Educational Psychology*, 98(3), 554; National Reading Panel (US), National Institute of Child Health, Human Development (US), National Reading Excellence Initiative, National Institute for Literacy (US), United States. Public Health Service, & United States Department of Health (2000). *Report of the National Reading Panel: Teaching children to read: An evidence-based assessment of the scientific research literature on reading and its implications for reading instruction: Reports of the subgroups*. National Institute of Child Health and Human Development, National Institutes of Health.
2 Nagy, W. E. and Herman, P. A. (1987). Breadth and depth of vocabulary knowledge: Implications for acquisition and instruction. In McKeown, M. G. and Curtis, M. E. (eds), The nature of vocabulary acquisition. Mahwah, NJ: Lawrence Erlbaum Associates, 19–35.
3 Gough, P. B., Hoover, W. A. and Peterson, C. L. (1996). Some observations on a simple view of reading. In Cornoldi, C. and Oakhill, J. (eds), *Reading Comprehension Difficulties: Processes and Intervention*. Mahwah, NJ: Lawrence Erlbaum Associates, 1–13; Ouellette (2006).
4 Nagy, W. E. and Scott, J. (2000). Vocabulary processes. In Kamil, M., Mosenthal, P., Pearson, P. D. and Barr, R. (eds), *Handbook of Reading Research* (Vol. 3). Mahwah, NJ: Lawrence Erlbaum Associates, 269–284; Cunningham, A. E. (2005). Vocabulary growth through independent reading and reading aloud to children. In Hiebert, E. H. and Kamhi, M. L. (eds), *Teaching and Learning Vocabulary: Bringing Research to Practice*. Mahwah, NJ: Lawrence Erlbaum Associates, 45–68.
5 Willingham, D. T. (2017). *The Reading Mind: A Cognitive Approach to Understanding How the Mind Reads*. Hoboken, NJ: John Wiley & Sons.
6 Stanovich, K. E. (2009). Matthew effects in reading: Some consequences of individual differences in the acquisition of literacy. *Journal of Education*, 189(1–2), 23–55.
7. Swanborn, M. S. and De Glopper, K. (1999). Incidental word learning while reading: A meta-analysis. *Review of Educational Research*, 69(3), 261–285.
8 Nagy and Herman (1987).
9 McGuinness, D. (2006). *Early Reading Instruction: What Science Really Tells Us About How to Teach Reading*. Cambridge, MA: MIT Press.
10 Cunningham (2005).
11 Seidenberg, M. (2017). *Language at the Speed of Sight: How We Read, Why So Many Can't, and What Can Be Done About It*. New York: Basic Books, 111.

12 Beck, I. L., McKeown, M. G. and Kucan, L. (2013). *Bringing Words to Life: Robust Vocabulary Instruction*. New York: Guilford Press.

13 Coxhead, A. (2000). A new academic word list. *TESOL Quarterly*, 34(2), 213–238.

14 Leech, G. and Rayson, P. (2014). *Word Frequencies in Written and Spoken English: Based on the British National Corpus*. London: Routledge; Longman (2007). *Longman Communication 3000*. Harlow: Pearson Longman.

15 Plaut, D. C. and Gonnerman, L. M. (2000). Are non-semantic morphological effects incompatible with a distributed connectionist approach to lexical processing? *Language and Cognitive Processes*, 15(4–5), 445–485; Rastle, K. and Davis, M. H. (2008). Morphological decomposition based on the analysis of orthography. *Language and Cognitive Processes*, 23(7–8), 942–971.

16 Liben, D. (2020). The importance of vocabulary and knowledge in comprehension. In Patterson, J. (ed.), *The SAT Suite and Classroom Practice: English Language Arts/ Literacy*. New York: College Board, 53–69.

17 Nagy, W. E., Carlisle, J. F. and Goodwin, A. P. (2014). Morphological knowledge and literacy acquisition. *Journal of Learning Disabilities*, 47(1), 3–12; Oakhill, J., Cain, K. and Elbro, C. (2019). Reading comprehension and reading comprehension difficulties. In Kilpatrick, D. A., Joshi, R. M. and Wagner, R. K. (eds), *Reading Development and Difficulties*. Cham: Springer International Publishing, 83–116.

18 Castles, A., Rastle, K. and Nation, K. (2018). Ending the reading wars: Reading acquisition from novice to expert. *Psychological Science in the Public Interest*, 19(1), 5–51.

19 Goodwin, A. P. and Ahn, S. (2013). A meta-analysis of morphological interventions in English: Effects on literacy outcomes for school-age children. *Scientific Studies of Reading*, 17(4), 257–285.

20 Masterson, J., Stuart, M., Dixon, M. and Lovejoy, S. (2010). Children's printed word database: Continuities and changes over time in children's early reading vocabulary. *British Journal of Psychology*, 101(2), 221–242.

21 Green, T. M. (2020). *The Greek & Latin Roots of English*. Lanham, MD: Rowman & Littlefield Publishers.

22 Rasinski, T., Padak, N., Newton, R. M. and Newton, E. (2008). *Greek and Latin Roots: Keys to Building Vocabulary*. Huntington Bech, CA: Shell Education.

23 Crosson, A. C. and McKeown, M. G. (2016). Middle school learners' use of Latin roots to infer the meaning of unfamiliar words. *Cognition and Instruction*, 34(2), 148–171.

24 Biemiller, A. (2010). *Words Worth Teaching: Closing the Vocabulary Gap*. Columbus, OH: McGraw-Hill SRA.

25 Zimmerman, L. and Reed, D. K. (2017). *Attributes of Effective Explicit Vocabulary Instruction*. Iowa Reading Research Center. Available at: https://iowareadingresearch. org/blog/vocabulary-instruction-part-2 (accessed 30 November 2020); Marulis, L. M. and Neuman, S. B. (2013). How vocabulary interventions affect young children at risk: A meta-analytic review. *Journal of Research on Educational Effectiveness*, 6(3), 223–262; Silverman, R. D., Proctor, C. P., Harring, J. R., Doyle, B., Mitchell, M. A. and Meyer, A. G. (2013). Teachers' instruction and students' vocabulary and comprehension: An exploratory study with English monolingual and Spanish-English bilingual students in grades 3–5. *Reading Research Quarterly*, 49, 31–60. doi:10.1002/rrq.63; Nash, H. and Snowling, M. (2006). Teaching new words to children with poor existing vocabulary knowledge: A controlled evaluation of the definition and context methods. *International Journal of Language & Communication Disorders*, 41(3), 335–354; Beck, McKeown and Kucan (2013).

12

BACKGROUND KNOWLEDGE

Our understanding of vocabulary is intimately linked to our knowledge of the world; it is impossible to know exactly where our grasp of a word's meaning ends and our **background knowledge** begins.[1] (Background knowledge is the knowledge gained from the sum of our worldly experiences.) For example, consider your understanding of the word 'tree'. Naturally, you can visualise different species, you can recognise the difference between evergreen and deciduous trees and you can bring to mind the different parts of trees, from the trunk to the leaves to the roots. Now, which part of this understanding is *vocabulary depth* relating to the word 'tree', and which part of this is just your *background knowledge*? As you can see, the two are impossible to unravel. In fact, when it comes to comprehension, some even see measures of background knowledge as merely being a proxy for measures of vocabulary.[2] Due to this intimate link between the two, it would be foolish to present background knowledge as somehow detached from vocabulary. For the purposes of this chapter, background knowledge is discussed in the same way as it is in the research literature: as an attempt to quantify a person's overall knowledge of a given context to which a text refers.

There is strong evidence to suggest that a reader's background knowledge supports their ability to extract information from a text, to make necessary inferences and consequently to construct and update a situation model (i.e. comprehend meaning).[3] As a result, too little knowledge of the subject to which a text relates can become a barrier to comprehension.[4] This is all very obvious, but it is still worth discussing as recognition of the importance of background knowledge isn't reflected in the reading curriculum that children receive in many schools.

If it is beyond doubt that children are supported in their reading by knowing lots about the world, then what are the implications for how we teach reading?

First, the learning that children undertake beyond discrete reading sessions is still part of their reading curriculum. When a child learns about deforestation in geography or electrical circuits in science, they are de facto improving their ability to read. More dots have been added to their pointillist canvas. This is just another reason why children deserve to learn a carefully sequenced curriculum full of knowledge that has been purposefully chosen, with worthwhile links within subjects and between them.

Second, all of the books and texts that are chosen for children to read should focus on worthwhile content, be they rich, captivating stories or non-fiction texts that help children discover something important about their world. This often means understanding the developmental stage of children. A text for 7-year-olds that discusses the exact function of white blood cells may seem ambitious, but if the class don't yet understand blood's role in the circulatory system, then the text would likely be an unwise choice. Equally, it may be tempting to teach children about the supercontinent of Pangea, but if they don't know about the continents as they currently exist, then learning about these should come first. Some concepts are simply more fundamental than others.

In summary, we must take every opportunity to develop our students' understanding of the world in which they live. Learning about our world and its culture *is* learning to read.

In a nutshell …

- Teach reading using texts that are chosen for the quality and relevance of their content.
- Ensure that children learn about their world from a coherent and carefully constructed curriculum.

Other implications for the classroom

This chapter has discussed the idea of children learning content that is considered to be worthwhile. Curriculum development is a vast area, and not one that can be sufficiently addressed in this book. Nonetheless, it is worth noting that ongoing selection and integration of the content of the curriculum should be a high priority for every school, not least because of the effects that it can have on children's reading comprehension abilities. In brief, the knowledge and skills to be learned by children should be chosen based on the value they bring to children's understanding of the world. It should align with a school's overall sense of purpose and be ordered in such a way that what is learned is retrieved for a purpose and connected to the rest of the curriculum. Constructing a curriculum involves difficult choices. Inevitably, much that is of value will be left untaught by any curriculum, but a school that considers and can justify its curriculum is far more likely to offer children the learning that they deserve and, as a significant bonus, support their ability to comprehend what they read.

—————————— Questions for professional discussions ——————————

- What examples of academic learning can you think of that are clearly distinct from children's grasp of vocabulary?
- What examples of academic learning can you think of that are impossible to untangle from children's grasp of vocabulary?
- What might be the advantages and disadvantages of a school selecting texts for reading lessons that closely match aspects of its broader curriculum?

—————————————— Retrieval quiz ——————————————

1 How does children's background knowledge contribute to their reading comprehension?
2 Why do some consider background knowledge to be a proxy for the extent of their vocabulary?

Further reading

- Aitchison, J. (2012). *Words in the Mind: An Introduction to the Mental Lexicon*. Hoboken, NJ: John Wiley & Sons.
- Wiliam, D. (2013). *Principled Curriculum Design*. London: SSAT (The Schools Network) Limited.

References

1 Aitchison, J. (2012). *Words in the Mind: An Introduction to the Mental Lexicon*. Hoboken, NJ: John Wiley & Sons.
2 Moje, E. B., Afflerbach, P. P., Enciso, P. and Lesaux, N. K. (2020). *Handbook of Reading Research, Volume V*. New York: Routledge.
3 Kintsch, W. (1988). The role of knowledge in discourse comprehension: A construction-integration model. *Psychological Review*, 95(2), 163; Barnes, M. A., Dennis, M. and Haefele-Kalvaitis, J. (1996). The effects of knowledge availability and knowledge accessibility on coherence and elaborative inferencing in children from six to fifteen years of age. *Journal of Experimental Child Psychology*, 61(3), 216–241; Recht, D. R. and Leslie, L. (1988). Effect of prior knowledge on good and poor readers' memory of text.

Journal of Educational Psychology, 80(1), 16; Liben, D. (2020). The importance of vocabulary and knowledge in comprehension. In Patterson, J. (ed.), *The SAT® Suite and Classroom Practice: English Language Arts/Literacy*. New York: College Board, 53–69.

4   O'Reilly, T., Wang, Z. and Sabatini, J. (2019). How much knowledge is too little? When a lack of knowledge becomes a barrier to comprehension. *Psychological Science*, 30(9), 1344–1351.

13

HOW THE ELEMENTS OF LANGUAGE COMPREHENSION INTERACT

In the previous chapters, I have discussed in isolation the different elements that support comprehension through the development of a situation model for a text: comprehension monitoring, inference, text structure, vocabulary and background knowledge. However, this compartmentalisation is merely a simplification used for the purposes of clarity. In reality, all of the elements of language comprehension reinforce one another and the boundary between one element and another is rarely clear cut.[1] In this chapter, I will briefly describe some of the ways that these different elements interact by looking at two elements of reading comprehension and how they are inextricably linked to the rest.

Comprehension monitoring

As we have seen, the metacognitive process of monitoring one's own comprehension is a strategy that children can be supported to use with relatively little teaching. It operates through reference to all of the other elements of comprehension:

- Comprehension monitoring can reveal where an *inference* may need to be made, perhaps because we are unsure to whom or what a pronoun is referring.
- Knowledge of the *text structure* can reveal that our comprehension is lacking, for example when it seems a character has acted in an unexpected way in a narrative.

- Noticing unknown *vocabulary* – and perhaps using morphology or contextual clues to deduce its meaning – is a crucial part of comprehension monitoring.
- Useful *background knowledge* may alert us to the fact that our comprehension has gone momentarily awry. For example, if in a story we believe that the main character – a customer in a shop – has opened the till, it is only our knowledge of how shops usually operate that helps us to realise that we may have made an error in our comprehension and need to read back. (We may not have made an error. Perhaps the main character has decided to take to a life of crime. However, it is our knowledge of commercial conventions that lets us know that this is unexpected and requires our attention if we are not to be misled.)

Inference

Inference is intimately connected to the other elements of language comprehension:

- The potential need for inferences can be provoked by our active *comprehension monitoring*.
- A *text's structure* may inform the type of inferences we may need to make. For example, the exact same words that seem appropriate in a formal letter may seem tellingly distant in a note to a close friend.
- Inference is impossible without secure *vocabulary* and *background knowledge* of the text being read.

It suffices to say that language comprehension must be considered as a single complex system. This is not to say that at points particular elements of language comprehension can't be taught in isolation. On the contrary, this may well be beneficial. However, it does mean that apparent difficulties in one area of comprehension might be the result of difficulties in another. When a child struggles to monitor their comprehension, it might be the result of vocabulary deficits or a lack of background knowledge relating to the text. An apparent inability to make inferences might relate to a child's poor grasp of pronouns; equally, it might simply be the result of an unfamiliar text structure or a weak grasp of comprehension monitoring. All of the elements of language comprehension reinforce one another. The same is true of decoding. Let's return briefly to the simple view of reading:

Decoding (D) × Language Comprehension (LC) = Reading Comprehension (RC)

Here we see that reading comprehension, the ultimate goal of reading, results in the interaction of not only all of the elements of language comprehension discussed in this section of the book, but also the interaction between these elements and decoding. A child's inability to develop a situation model for a text, and thus comprehend it, is just as often the result of struggles with decoding as it is to do with a weakness in one of the elements of language comprehension. All reading teachers need to be aware of the complex nature of reading so that insufficient understanding can be recognised and teaching can be adapted as a result.

Assessment

The assessment of a student's ability to comprehend is often undertaken through the use of standardised tests, which are readily available (at a price) to schools. There are strong arguments that reading comprehension tests (including the end-of-school reading assessment in England) do not validly assess what they purport to, namely generic reading comprehension skills.[2] This makes sense given that there is scant evidence that such skills even exist. Just as reading comprehension is reliant upon fluent decoding, vocabulary, background knowledge and knowledge of text structure and syntax, so comprehension tests inevitably end up assessing these elements. This is not to say that comprehension tests are valueless. Used alongside fluency assessments (and phonics assessments where necessary), standardised comprehension scores can indicate which children are struggling to comprehend despite age-appropriate reading fluency; this can inform teaching and, in rare cases, intervention. Nevertheless, in my experience, a significant majority of children who struggle on tests of comprehension do so because of issues relating to reading fluency. Accordingly, fluency assessments tend to provide more useful information about children's reading attainment than assessments of reading comprehension.

――――――――――――――――――― In a nutshell … ―――――――――――――――――――

- Recognise the interaction between all the elements of language comprehension (and between these elements and decoding) so that teaching can be responsive.
- Understand that deficiencies in reading comprehension are *not* best tackled by the teaching of generic 'comprehension skills' such as predicting and making inferences.
- Teach all of the elements of language comprehension. (See Chapter 21 for more on this.)

Other implications for the classroom

In the complexity of real classrooms, it can be tempting to simplify the reading difficulties of a child down to just one element that is lacking: 'He struggles with reading just because of a narrow vocabulary. She struggles with reading because her phonics is weak.' While there may often be useful truth in such statements, it is important to bear in mind that children who struggle with reading comprehension are likely to have weaknesses across multiple areas. Often, teachers will support children to develop one area of their reading capabilities and then be disappointed to see that a transformation in outcomes hasn't materialised for the child. Knowing about the complex, interacting nature of the elements of language comprehension can help us to remember that support given may not be reflected in immediate outcomes, but might still be an essential step towards the child's eventual improvement.

_____ Questions for professional discussions _____

- Given what we know about reading assessments, is there still value in using them to assess the reading ability of children who we know have significant weaknesses in their decoding ability?
- Would a reading comprehension test where the subject matter was known well by some students provide a useful indicator of their reading ability? Would an equivalent test where none of the subject matter was known well be better? What does this show about the information acquired by teachers from comprehension tests?

_____ Retrieval quiz _____

1 Give three ways in which comprehension monitoring can interact with other elements of language comprehension.
2 Give three ways in which inference can interact with other elements of language comprehension.

Further reading

- Oakhill, J., Cain, K. and Elbro, C. (2014). *Understanding and Teaching Reading Comprehension: A Handbook*. London: Routledge.

References

1 Oakhill, J., Cain, K. and Elbro, C. (2014). *Understanding and Teaching Reading Comprehension: A Handbook*. London; Routledge.
2 *Reforming the Key Stage 2 Reading SAT – Why It's Needed and Possible.* Teachwell, 3 May. Available at: www.teach-well.com/reforming-the-key-stage-2-reading-sat-why-its-needed-and-possible/ (accessed 30 November 2020).

Part IV

Opportunities to Enhance Reading

14

INDEPENDENT READING/ READING FOR PLEASURE

The amount of reading that children do outside of school varies enormously. Estimates, dated though they admittedly are, suggest that the most voracious readers among 10-year-olds read more than 4 million words per year, nearly 100 times the amount of other readers the same age.[1] This extra experience contributes to one example of the aforementioned 'Matthew effect' – through which stronger readers read more words, and reading more words makes them stronger readers – a virtuous cycle that inevitably widens the achievement gap.[2] In fact, despite our responsibility to teach reading to a high standard in the classroom, the transition from novice to expert reader ultimately requires independent reading.[3] As children become fluent readers, listening is surpassed by reading as the primary means through which they gain new understanding of words and grammar. Thus, this difference in the amount of independent reading undertaken doesn't only have an impact on a child's reading ability; it potentially has an impact on their oral language capabilities as well.[4] In short, our success in helping children to become expert readers partly depends on their willingness to read independently.

So, how can we support this? It's tempting to think that finding ways to directly reward reading might be beneficial, for example through the giving of prizes for regular reading. However, Willingham (2017) is not alone in suggesting that extrinsic motivation has the potential to backfire, reducing children's desire to read over the long term as rewards imply that reading is something not worth doing for its own sake.[5] This is not to say that it is wrong for children to associate reading with something pleasurable, such as quality time spent with a parent/carer, but this association should be inherent to the reading experience itself. Fortunately, there are other ways that reading can be encouraged. Over my career these are some of the ways that I have seen have positive impacts.

Read aloud to children

No matter how the school day goes, time for reading aloud should be sacrosanct. I have lost count of the number of times that, having read a book to the class, reluctant readers have approached me and asked for a copy. Re-reading a book where the plot is understood and the characters have already been brought to life by a teacher can be a great first step into independent reading for reluctant readers. In addition, adding extra reading time as a treat sends a powerful message about the enjoyment that can be derived from books.

Make time for independent reading

It can be hard to make time for children to read independently in a packed school curriculum. Nevertheless, many children's home environments are not conducive to independent reading, and thus schools should try to provide this opportunity, even if it is only for a short time each day. Of course, such opportunities are only of benefit to those who have developed a level of reading fluency that allows them to enjoy independent reading; those who have not will simply embed their dysfluency or, just as likely, will pretend to read during this part of the school day and begin to associate reading with a sense of shame. For this reason, daily independent reading time is only suitable for classes in which the majority can read books with the fluency required to derive meaning and enjoyment. In such classes, this time is a chance for teachers to work with those who need further support. Where every child in a class is able to enjoy independent reading, the teacher can join the children in reading silently, modelling a love of books and helping to nurture a reading community within the classroom.

Have accessible reading corners in classrooms or school libraries

Teachers sometimes create welcoming spaces for reading without considering how accessible the books are. For example, too many books can be daunting for children, and too few can be restrictive. Giving children the responsibility as class librarians to keep the books ordered can be a great way to show that reading is a priority in your school.

Recommend books to children

Few things motivate reading as much as an adult taking the time to consider a child's personality and interests and making a recommendation on this basis.

Naturally, this does not mean limiting a child's reading material or giving them books that fit some stereotype of what kids 'like them' *should* be interested in. By gaining their trust with books you suspect will match their interests, you give yourself the opportunity to challenge them later with something that may expand their horizons.

Allow children to change books if they are unconvinced

This requires a delicate balance and a sharp eye. Reluctant readers will often spend precious reading time constantly changing books. In the end, it is important that they make a commitment to read one to its conclusion. However, this is not to say that *every* book needs to be finished. Giving children the freedom to occasionally give up on a book implicitly tells them that reading can and should feel worthwhile.

Ensure there are plenty of quality non-fiction texts available

Quality non-fiction books are often much harder to find in classrooms than stories, and yet many children prefer to read them. No reading corner or school library is complete without a varied supply of non-fiction.

Do not discourage children from taking home a book, regardless of its difficulty

In the earliest stages of reading, children need to practise decoding using the sound–spelling correspondences that they have learned. This does not mean that they shouldn't in addition be taking home other books for enjoyment with their family. As they get older, it can become harder for children to find books that suit their current reading ability. Some schools use a book-banding system to support children in finding books that they can enjoy independently or practise reading from with adult support. Such systems suffer from a bad reputation, though I think this relates to how they are used rather than the systems themselves. It can be valuable to use a book-banding system with older children to help busy teachers recommend books and to ensure children have a book that they can read to a parent/carer with at least some success in decoding. It is *not* valuable, however, to have a book-banding system that ever prevents children from taking home a particular book because it is 'too hard' or 'too easy'. It is essential that children have the right to take home any book they please from a classroom reading corner or school library.

Ensure that books represent the diversity of the school and wider society

Children have the right to read books that reflect them, their lives and the community in which they live. Classrooms and school libraries must play their part in this.

Be a reading role model

Find any excuse to discuss the reading you do and the value it has. Explain that sometimes it can be a struggle to find something you want to read, but emphasise that the effort is always worth it in the end. This can provide encouragement to reluctant readers.

Prioritise reading with parents/carers over any other form of homework

Many busy parents/carers have limited time for homework. Where possible, ensure that reading at home is prioritised. Parents/carers can also be supported to encourage productive reading habits, such as the decoding of unfamiliar words.

Teach reading well

While the above suggestions can each make a small contribution to a child's motivation to read independently, they will all be for nothing if the child in question hasn't developed the ability to read fluently. Teaching children to read well is *by far* the most significant thing that any teacher can do to encourage independent reading and a love of books.[6]

—————————————— In a nutshell … ——————————————

- Avoid extrinsic rewards for reading.
- Consider how to implement the strategies discussed above in your context.
- Ensure that the teaching of reading has the best chance of being effective by basing your practice on a sensible interpretation of the reading science outlined in this book.

Other implications for the classroom

One of the greatest challenges of developing independent readers is knowing how to support children who struggle with phonics or fluency despite having been at school for several years. Providing appropriate reading material for these children is difficult as the books that match their decoding ability often don't have the sort of content that is appropriate or interesting for their age range. The reality is that these children are very unlikely to read independently at home. In almost all cases, the only route to independent reading is via a long slog through guided supported reading with a supportive adult. Consequently, these children are better off with books that suit their age range in terms of content rather than those that match their independent ability to decode. Yes, where necessary, these children may still need practice with phonically controlled books (see Chapter 4). Nevertheless, my experience suggests that as soon as they are moving beyond these, they are better off reading to an adult for at least five minutes a day from a challenging text than being expected to read from something they might find easier but that doesn't offer the prize of interesting content as they begin to progress. In short, independent reading is of limited use to readers who are still struggling with the basics of phonics or fluency. Targeted adult support is required to support their development.

It is important to be honest with children. Those who are struggling to decode will think little of our views if we tell them what a joyous experience reading should be for them already. The all-too-familiar reality for these children is that reading is a chore. Why? Because for them the process of reading is slow, awkward and often linked in a negative way to their self-esteem. The best thing to do in this situation is to explain to children that reading *will* be a chore for a while as they slowly get better at it, but that – like any skill – it will become far more rewarding as they improve. In the meantime, the satisfaction in reading needs to be gained from a sense of progression rather than from the content of books alone, something that a teacher can provide through feedback and encouragement.

—————————— Questions for professional discussions ——————————

- Given that children pick up on subtle signals about whether a task is worth undertaking on its own merits, what are the advantages and disadvantages of praising children for reading regularly?
- What alternative encouragement might be available to teachers?

—————————————— Retrieval quiz ——————————————

1   Why might it not be a good idea to reward children for reading independently?
2   Give four ways that independent reading can be encouraged?

Further reading

- Willingham, D. T. (2017). *The Reading Mind: A Cognitive Approach to Understanding How the Mind Reads.* Hoboken, NJ: John Wiley & Sons.

References

1   Castles, A., Rastle, K. and Nation, K. (2018). Ending the reading wars: Reading acquisition from novice to expert. *Psychological Science in the Public Interest*, 19(1), 5–51.
2   Stanovich, K. E. (2009). Matthew effects in reading: Some consequences of individual differences in the acquisition of literacy. *Journal of Education*, 189(1–2), 23–55.
3   Willingham, D. T. (2017). *The Reading Mind: A Cognitive Approach to Understanding How the Mind Reads*. Hoboken, NJ: John Wiley & Sons.
4   Seidenberg, M. (2017). *Language at the Speed of Sight: How We Read, Why So Many Can't, and What Can Be Done About It*. New York: Basic Books.
5   Willingham (2017); Lepper, M. R., Greene, D. and Nisbett, R. E. (1973). Undermining children's intrinsic interest with extrinsic reward: A test of the 'overjustification' hypothesis. *Journal of Personality and Social Psychology*, 28(1), 129.
6   Mol, S. E. and Bus, A. G. (2011). To read or not to read: a meta-analysis of print exposure from infancy to early adulthood. *Psychological Bulletin*, 137(2), 267.

15

READING ACROSS
THE CURRICULUM

One obvious way to help ensure that children undertake the large amount of reading that is required to build fluency and support comprehension is to embed reading
across the curriculum. There are two types of reading across the curriculum: **content
area reading** and **disciplinary reading**.[1]

Content area reading is any reading that supports children's grasp of the body of
knowledge related to a given school subject. For example, this may involve reading
an expository text about the festival of Diwali or an extract from the diary of Samuel
Pepys. The purpose is simply to learn more about the subject at hand, something that
can be done by children as soon as their reading ability allows. In contrast, disciplinary
reading involves content area reading, but it goes beyond this to engage children in a
deeper understanding of the subject itself. School subjects – history, mathematics, etc. –
are not merely limited versions of academic disciplines; school subjects are what is created from academic disciplines after they have been recontextualised by intermediar-
ies, such as government departments. This recontextualisation defines the scope and
order of what is to be taught in a school subject, at least to some extent.[2] Despite this,
the school subjects are still directly related to the academic disciplines. Each academic
discipline is defined by the *meaning it makes*, defined as **substantive knowledge**,
and by the *way in which it makes meaning*, defined as **disciplinary knowledge**.[3]
Disciplinary knowledge is the knowledge of how meaning in that discipline is gained,
how it is scrutinised and how it is revised. It is different for each of the academic disciplines. Disciplinary reading thus involves reading in a way that aligns with – and
illuminates – the disciplinary knowledge of a particular academic discipline.

What might this look like in practice? Let's take history and science as examples:

> The *substantive knowledge of history* is the knowledge of the past shared with students
> that is accepted as most likely to be factually accurate. The *disciplinary knowledge of*

history involves understanding what being a historian entails: the development of interpretations of past events based on the available evidence. It is inevitably informed by a perspective that gives weight to different evidence and prioritises different interpretations. Historians use interpretive frameworks to create coherent narratives about the past. As such, *disciplinary reading in history* focuses on sources, context and corroboration (i.e. Who or where is this evidence from? What were the influencing circumstances at the time? How does this evidence align with other available evidence?)[4]

The *substantive knowledge of science* is the knowledge of the natural world shared with students that is most likely to be factually accurate and relevant. The *disciplinary knowledge of science* involves understanding what being a scientist entails: the interpretation of empirical evidence to derive testable principles, called theories, that explain what we observe in the natural world. As a result, *disciplinary reading in science* focuses on methods, explanations and conclusions (i.e. How was this evidence derived? How is this evidence explained? What are the consequences if this explanation is accurate?)[5]

Disciplinary reading has a valuable role to play in supporting children's understanding of academic disciplines, revealing to them the different ways that people derive meaning from the world. This is not to suggest that children are equipped for this in the early stages of their reading journey. It might be the case that disciplinary reading is something that children undertake once their reading fluency is suitably advanced. Nevertheless, teachers, reading coordinators and those responsible for curriculum development more broadly should be aware of the potential of disciplinary reading to support children's reading development and to advance their understanding of the school subjects and the academic disciplines to which they relate.

––––––––––––––––––––––––––––––––— In a nutshell … —––––––––––––––––––––––––––––––––

- Take advantage of reading sessions as an opportunity for content area reading across the curriculum.
- Recognise the opportunity for disciplinary reading in other subjects as a way to support reading outcomes while developing knowledge of academic disciplines.

Other implications for the classroom

One of the most challenging aspects of educating younger children is that we have to be capable of teaching subjects from across the entire curriculum. This can mean that the time we have to develop our subject knowledge and the pedagogical knowledge related to a specific subject is spread thin. However, there are great advantages to having teachers that teach the same children for all subjects, not least when it comes to the teaching of reading. Teachers that integrate reading into lessons across the curriculum – and who integrate study of the entire curriculum into their reading lessons – are able to use their knowledge of the children to great effect. The reading in a geography lesson can involve fluency practice (see Chapter 21) if a class are struggling in this area. The texts selected in a reading lesson can prepare children for an aspect of science that the teacher knows children tend to find tricky. Everyone benefits when teachers are supported to see the entire curriculum, including reading lessons, as interconnected.

─────────── Questions for professional discussions ───────────

- What school subjects might be most conducive to disciplinary reading? Why?
- Are there any school subjects in which content area reading would provide little benefit? Why?

─────────── Retrieval quiz ───────────

1   What is the difference between content area reading and disciplinary reading?
2   What is the difference between substantive knowledge and disciplinary knowledge?

Further reading

- Shanahan, C. and Shanahan, T. (2020). Disciplinary literacy. In Patterson, J. (ed.) *The SAT® Suite and Classroom Practice: English Language Arts/Literacy*. New York: College Board, 91–125.

References

1   Shanahan, C. and Shanahan, T. (2020). Disciplinary literacy. In Patterson, J. (ed.), *The SAT® Suite and Classroom Practice: English Language Arts/Literacy*. New York: College Board, 91–125.
2   Ashbee, R. (2020). Why it's so important to understand school subjects – and how we might begin to do so. In Sealy, C. (ed.), *The ResearchED Guide to the Curriculum*. Woodbridge: John Catt, 31–40.
3   Counsell, C. (2018). Taking curriculum seriously. *Impact: Journal of the Chartered College of Teaching*, Issue 4. Available at: https://impact.chartered.college/article/taking-curriculum-seriously/ (accessed 7 January 2021).
4   Shanahan and Shanahan (2020).
5   Ibid.

16

WRITING

As we have seen, reading and writing can be considered as two sides of the same coin, so the teaching of reading and writing are inevitably mutually supportive. Consequently, there are elements within the teaching of writing that can be included or adapted to further assist children's reading acquisition.

Sentence-level work

Children's ability to make local cohesion inferences (see Chapter 9) partly depends on their grasp of **anaphors** and **connectives**. Anaphors are words or phrases that refer back to an earlier word or phrase. Pronouns can fulfil this role (e.g. 'Sameera's car was dirty so *she* washed *it*') as can adverbs (e.g. 'Jamie was hungry and *so was* I'). Connectives are words or phrases that link sentences and phrases. These can be conjunctions (e.g. 'but', 'so', 'while') or adverbs/adverbial phrases (e.g. 'nevertheless', 'as a result', 'meanwhile'). Ensuring that children grasp the meaning of anaphors and connectives in their writing will support their use of them as they read. One way to achieve this is to use the sentence stem activities advocated in *The Writing Revolution* by Judith Hochman and Natalie Wexler (2017).[1] However, the teaching of sentence structures and their components, while useful, should concentrate first on children's ability to comprehend the meaning behind their use; in my experience, teachers sometimes focus on children's ability to accurately *use* certain devices and sentence constructions before the children have *understood* what the devices mean in reading. This being the case, the priority remains to expose children to well-written texts containing these constructions before they attempt to use them in their own writing.[2]

Spelling

The teaching of spelling is intimately linked with the teaching of reading.[3] In fact, there is some evidence that spelling interventions are more effective at supporting struggling readers than interventions focused on reading.[4] Therefore, it is important that teachers recognise the value of teaching spelling and the particular ways of teaching spelling that support reading (and those that do the opposite):

- Limit children's exposure to inaccurate spellings: there is evidence to suggest that children should not be exposed to examples of misspelling as this can lead to an increase in mistakes later on. This means that activities where children pick the correct spelling from a list that includes inaccurate spellings is likely to be counter-productive. In addition, advising children to write out various possible spellings and then pick the one that looks correct, described as an 'anti-spelling method' by McGuinness (2006), is probably inadvisable for novice readers.[5]
- Avoid teaching spelling rules: as implied by the logic underpinning phonics (see Chapter 4), teaching children various spelling rules is unlikely to support their spelling or contribute positively to their reading.
- Ensure that spelling practice involves writing the word in question: it sounds obvious, but the process of writing letters supports remembering the spelling of words.[6] Activities that involve mere recognition of spellings, such as wordsearches, are unlikely to be effective (not to mention how inefficient such activities often are). For young children, saying the letters aloud as they spell may also support spelling and reading.[7]
- Support children to focus on the part of the word that is 'tricky', ensuring that the other sound–spelling correspondences are correct. For example, when spelling the word 'float', children can be fairly confident about the graphemes required to represent the /f/, /l/ and /t/ phonemes; this ensures that they can concentrate their mind on the remaining <oa> grapheme, which also helps teachers to focus their assistance on just a portion of a word.

Relating specific text structure to generalised text structure

Quality writing is often the result of quality modelling by a teacher. Sharing with children a model text allows them to see what success looks like. A valuable part of this process, one that supports children's understanding of text structure, is the relation of the parts of a specific text structure to a generalised text structure. For example, if children are to write an expository text that mirrors a modelled text about giraffes, it is useful for them to see the model text as a generalised structure:

Title → Brief introduction about the animal → Appearance and behaviour → Habitat → Diet…

In this way, children can use specific texts and their structures to learn generalised text structures that support their writing and their reading.

———————————————— In a nutshell … ————————————————

- Teach children how to use anaphors (including pronouns) and connectives *after* they have experienced them in texts.
- Limit children's exposure to inaccurate spellings and spelling rules.
- Focus spelling practice on writing, and encourage children to focus on the 'tricky' parts of words.
- Teach text structures by relating the specific structure of model texts to generalised text structures.

Other implications for the classroom

The teaching of grammar is a contentious issue in education. Teachers sometimes deride the seemingly arcane language that is thrust upon children, such as prepositional phrases and the subjunctive mood. I have often heard teachers say that they themselves learned to write without an explicit understanding of grammatical terminology and that this shows that there is no point in teaching it. Putting to one side the wildly varying standards of writing proficiency across the teaching profession, there are some important points to make on this subject. First, teachers are, on average, a fairly well-educated group; just because some of us became competent writers without a particular form of teaching does not mean that this teaching has no value for others. Second, a person could quite possibly become an expert mechanic without being able to name a single car part, but they would be severely limited in their ability to communicate with others about car maintenance. In the same way, a shared understanding of grammatical terminology allows us to talk about language, especially how it works and how to use it more effectively. This brings me nicely to the key point about teaching grammar: it is a tool. Children need to know about subjects, verbs and conjunctions precisely because this allows them to discuss the construction of sentences in English, and any other language for that matter. Grammar teaching is often maligned because it is detached from this underlying purpose. In brief, it is well worth teachers grasping the fundamentals of grammar and the related terminology so that we can support children to understand, discuss and ultimately master the nuances of their language. Should this involve asking 7-year-olds to identify the subjunctive mood in a sentence? Certainly not. However, a child who knows, for example, how subjects and verbs work together is taking an important step towards mastering the written language and making it their own, something that will support their reading as much as it does their writing.

———————— Questions for professional discussions ————————

- What grammatical terminology – if any – is it essential for children to understand when they first begin to write and edit full sentences?
- What are the advantages of showing children generalised text structures for different texts? What are the disadvantages and how might these be minimised?

———————— Retrieval quiz ————————

1   What are anaphors?
2   Give three ways that spelling can be taught in a way that supports reading.

Further reading

- Hochman, J. C. and Wexler, N. (2017). *The Writing Revolution: A Guide to Advancing Thinking Through Writing in All Subjects and Grades*. San Francisco, CA: Jossey-Bass.
- McGuinness, D. (2006). *Early Reading Instruction: What Science Really Tells Us About How to Teach Reading*. Cambridge, MA: MIT Press.

References

1   Hochman, J. C. and Wexler, N. (2017). *The Writing Revolution: A Guide to Advancing Thinking Through Writing in All Subjects and Grades*. San Francisco, CA: Jossey-Bass.
2   Oakhill, J., Cain, K. and Elbro, C. (2014). *Understanding and Teaching Reading Comprehension. A Handbook*. London: Routledge.
3   Shanahan, T. (1984). Nature of the reading-writing relation: An exploratory multivariate analysis. *Journal of Educational Psychology. 76*, 466–477.
4   Uhry, J. K. and Shepherd, M. J. (1993). Segmentation/spelling instruction as part of a first-grade reading program: Effects on several measures of reading. *Reading Research Quarterly. 28*, 219–233.
5   McGuinness, D. (2006). *Early Reading Instruction: What Science Really Tells Us About How to Teach Reading*. MIT Press.
6   Cunningham, A. E. and Stanovich, K. E. (1990). Early spelling acquisition: Writing beats the computer. *Journal of Educational Psychology, 82*, 159–162.
7   Walker, J. (2019, February 10). *Super-Charged Phonics*. The Literacy Blog. https://theliteracyblog.com/2019/02/10/super-charged-phonics/

Part V

Addressing Reading Difficulties

17

DYSLEXIA

What is dyslexia?

Dyslexia is a term that is subject to a great deal of debate. This is not surprising given that there isn't a universally accepted definition of dyslexia. Nevertheless, it *is* widely agreed that dyslexia relates to difficulty in word reading that has genetic, neurobiological causes, i.e. causes relating to the brain's structure due to people's unique biology.[1] (To be more precise, difficulties in word reading that are related to initial learning are termed *developmental dyslexia*; those related to dyslexia caused by brain injury *after* learning to read are termed *acquired dyslexia*. For the remainder of this chapter, where the term 'dyslexia' is used, this will refer to *developmental dyslexia*.) Where word-reading difficulties are believed to be wholly caused by environmental factors, this is rarely described as dyslexia, though the exact causes of word-reading difficulties can be hard to unravel as the effects of environment and genetics are inevitably intertwined.[2] Previously, dyslexia was defined by researchers as a significant discrepancy between a person's reading abilities and their IQ. This discrepancy model has been disputed and is no longer seen as a valid means of defining dyslexia.[3] In short, dyslexia can be thought of as an extreme difficulty in word reading that has causes that are not purely environmental.

What are the underlying causes of dyslexia?

There is likely no single cause of the word-reading difficulties described as dyslexia. There is, as Wolf (2008) states, 'no one form of dyslexia; instead, there is a continuum of developmental reading disabilities that reflects the many components of reading, as well as the specific writing system in a given language' (p. 324).[4] However, it *is* the case that those with extreme word-level reading difficulties seem to invariably have weaknesses that relate to phonological processing in some form.[5] Decades of research trying to find causal links to other explanations (such as visual processing impairments) has resulted in precious little.[6] Dyslexia is correlated with greater likelihood of speech and language disorders, ADHD (attention-deficit hyperactivity disorder) and maths impairments, but it seems that phonological impairments of various kinds are the most likely cause of the word-reading difficulties that are labelled as dyslexia.[7]

What disagreement exists about the use of 'dyslexia' as a label for word-reading difficulties?

There is no clear delineation between people who are dyslexic and those that struggle with word reading to an extent that doesn't quite meet the threshold for diagnosis. People with dyslexia are merely those at the extreme of a normal distribution in terms of their difficulty in learning to decode words and/or read words fluently.[8] As a result, some argue that dividing all readers into two categories – those with dyslexia and those without – gives an inaccurate impression about the distribution of reading difficulties and leads to inefficient use of resources to support reading in schools.[9]

McGuinness (2006) argues that all reading difficulties in English are the result of 'the English spelling system and the way it is taught' (p. 3), her reasoning being that 'for a biological theory to be accurate, dyslexia would have to occur at the same rate in all populations' (p. 3).[10] Obviously, this is inaccurate. It is perfectly possible for a biologically caused difficulty with word reading that is prevalent across all populations to disproportionately manifest itself where orthography is particularly opaque; it is not uncommon for the effects of genetic predispositions to manifest themselves more frequently, or solely, in specific environments. Regardless, McGuinness's underlying rationale for making this point is sound and worth repeating: the vast majority of word-reading difficulties *are* likely avoidable with high-quality reading instruction, regardless of whether the difficulties are biological in origin. The English language is particularly tricky to decode, providing almost unique challenges for children and requiring a great deal of persistence.

How should children defined as having dyslexia be supported?

Seidenberg (2017) points out that assigning the label of dyslexia to word-reading difficulties is the 'purposeful medicalization of normal behaviour' (p. 158) akin to the diagnosis of hypertension and obesity.[11] (It is important to note that 'normal' here means 'part of a normal distribution' rather than 'average'.) While he is right to point out that dyslexia requires 'explicit, targeted' support, in my experience it is common for education professionals to interpret such 'medicalization' as suggesting that children with dyslexia require qualitatively different reading support than others. Crucially, this is not the case.[12] Those defined as dyslexic require the exact same type of support as all struggling readers, though this support may require greater commitment of time and effort from all involved. This support should reflect the areas where the individual learner is struggling, and is likely to comprise high-quality phonics teaching including phonemic manipulation, reading practice and/or fluency activities.

As Wolf (2008) states, 'it is ultimately of no consequence what we call the brain's inability to acquire reading' (p. 280).[13] What matters to children, parents/carers, teachers and schools is that those who exhibit extreme word-reading difficulties are supported by quality teaching in class and by further intervention where required. This is every school's responsibility, regardless of whether an individual child is defined as having dyslexia or not.

In a nutshell …

- Understand that when a child struggles far more than most with word reading, whether or not they are defined as dyslexic should not make a qualitative difference to the support they receive: they require timely, focused support relating to the aspects of word reading with which they struggle; this is likely to involve high-quality phonics teaching involving phoneme manipulation and/or fluency practice.

Other implications for the classroom

Dyslexia is an exceptionally sensitive subject. The label of dyslexia has provided enormous relief to countless people, including parents/carers who feel that a diagnosis of dyslexia will give access to extra support that would otherwise be unavailable. In terms of conversations with parents/carers and colleagues, it is always best to direct conversations around dyslexia towards the aspects upon which everyone can agree: the importance of quality reading instruction – the same kind that benefits all children – and the quantitative differences that might be required for the child in question to learn to read.

Questions for professional discussions

- How important is it for there to be a clear, shared understanding of dyslexia across a school?
- What might be the consequences if parents/carers receive different messages on the subject from different members of staff?

———————————————— Retrieval quiz ————————————————

1   What is the difference between developmental dyslexia and acquired dyslexia?
2   What other conditions are correlated with a diagnosis of dyslexia?
3   What differences might there be in the reading instruction for a child diagnosed with dyslexia compared to another child with less significant word-reading difficulties? Are these differences qualitative or quantitative?

Further reading

- Kilpatrick, D. A., Joshi, R. M. and Wagner, R. K. (eds) (2019). *Reading Development and Difficulties*. Cham: Springer International Publishing.

References

1   Wolf, M. (2008). *Proust and the Squid: The Story and Science of the Reading Brain*. New York: Harper Perennial, 147–148; Snowling, M. J. and Hulme, C. E. (2005). *The Science of Reading: A Handbook* (Blackwell Handbooks of Developmental Psychology). Oxford: Blackwell Publishing.
2   Seidenberg, M. (2017). *Language at the Speed of Sight: How We Read, Why So Many Can't, and What Can Be Done About It*. New York: Basic Books.
3   Tanaka, H., Black, J. M., Hulme, C., Stanley, L. M., Kesler, S. R., Whitfield-Gabrieli, S., ... and Hoeft, F. (2011). The brain basis of the phonological deficit in dyslexia is independent of IQ. *Psychological Science*, 22(11), 1442–1451.
4   Wolf (2008), 324.
5   Kilpatrick, D. and O'Brien, S. (2019). Effective prevention and intervention for word-level reading difficulties. In Kilpatrick, D. A., Joshi, R. M. and Wagner, R. K. (eds), *Reading Development and Difficulties*. Cham: Springer International Publishing, 179–212.
6   Ahmed, Y., Wagner, R. K. and Thatcher Kantor, P. (2012). How visual word recognition is affected by developmental dyslexia. *Visual Word Recognition*, 2, 196–215; Vellutino, F. R., Fletcher, J. M., Snowling, M. J. and Scanlon, D. M. (2004). Specific reading disability (dyslexia): What have we learned in the past four decades? *Journal of Child Psychology and Psychiatry*, 45(1), 2–40; Fletcher, J. M., Lyon, G. R., Fuchs, L. S. and Barnes, M. A. (2018). *Learning Disabilities: From Identification to Intervention*. New York: Guilford Press.
7   Seidenberg (2017).
8   Ibid.; International Dyslexia Association. *Definition of Dyslexia*. Available at: https://dyslexiaida.org/definition-of-dyslexia/ (accessed 30 November 2020); Spinath, B. and Ramachandran, V. S. (2012). *Encyclopedia of Human Behaviour*. London: Academic Press.
9   Elliott, J. G. and Gibbs, S. (2008). Does dyslexia exist? *Journal of Philosophy of Education*, 42(3–4), 475–491.
10 McGuinness, D. (2006). *Early Reading Instruction: What Science Really Tells Us About How to Teach Reading*. Cambridge, MA: MIT Press, 3.
11 Seidenberg (2017), 158.
12 Kilpatrick and O'Brien (2019).
13 Wolf (2008), 280.

18

ASSESSMENT AND DATA

Naturally, individual teachers and schools need to have an appropriately accurate view of the current reading abilities of their students. As we have seen in previous chapters, phonics, fluency and reading comprehension can, and should, be monitored on a regular basis to ensure that children can be supported and that systemic strengths and weaknesses in the reading curriculum can be identified. But what data needs to be tracked? What information do we need to have available about each student?

First, every student in the school should have a phonics status, relating to their grasp of the phonics taught to them in the first two years of school. If a child has not mastered these aspects of the code, regardless of their year group, then this information should be tracked so that children have one of only two possible statuses: 'mastered this aspect of phonics' or 'continuing to learn this aspect of phonics'. For students further up the school, this may require systematic intervention. Children in English schools who do not pass the Year 1 phonics screening check will also need to be tracked to ensure that they are supported, ready for the re-assessment at the end of Year 2. (It is also worth reiterating here that the teaching of spelling that continues throughout school is based on phonics. Thus, phonics teaching isn't something that *ends*. It is something that *adapts*, so that children learn the various ways that particular sounds can be represented in different words.)

Second, the level of reading fluency for every student should be monitored, using the style of assessment outlined in Chapter 5. This means that every child in a school should have a words correct per minute (WCPM) score tracked alongside a teacher's assessment of that child's prosody. Once students reach a suitable level of fluency, say 110+ WCPM prosodic reading with an age-appropriate text, then it is no longer necessary to keep track of their exact fluency attainment.

Third, standardised reading comprehension tests can provide a reading age for each child that should also be tracked. As discussed in Chapter 13, this reading age will provide a generalised view of a child's ability to decode fluently alongside their vocabulary, background knowledge and understanding of sentence structure and text structure. A reading age is a suitably jargon-free, comprehensible piece of informa-tion for sharing with parents/carers so that they can understand their child's reading attainment. The information it provides is most useful alongside that from a fluency assessment in that it can indicate those readers that might benefit from brief support with comprehension strategies (i.e. fluent readers whose comprehension is relatively weak). Having said that, the best remediation for such poor comprehenders is likely to be lots of reading to support the development of their vocabulary, their knowledge of the world and their understanding of text and sentence structure. This may not be best achieved through intervention.

The only data that should be tracked by a reading coordinator for any area of learning is that which can be used to inform teaching. In the case of reading, the information in Table 18.1 fits that description.

Table 18.1 Example of data to inform teaching

Name	Year group	Phonics initial/basic code	Phonics screening check (most recent)	Phonics advanced code	Fluency (WCPM)	Fluency (prosody)	Reading age
Child A	3	√	38/40	√	76	√	7y 11m
Child B	3	√	34/40	√	67	x	7y 3m
Child C	2	√	39/40	developing	50	x	6y 7m
Child D	2	developing (intervention)	27/40	developing	24	x	n/a
Child E	1	developing	n/a	developing	n/a	x	n/a
Child F	1	developing	n/a	developing	n/a	x	n/a

More detailed results from phonics assessments that track children's ability to use the sounds already taught may also be useful to individual class teachers.

_____ In a nutshell ... _____

- Where appropriate, assess and track children's phonics, fluency and reading age via a standardised test.
- Only assess and track information that directly informs teaching over the short or long term.

Other implications for the classroom

Schools sometimes require their teachers to analyse children's grasp of reading against a long list of criteria, using this as a best-fit guide to children's reading attainment, referencing evidence to support the judgement for each child. Having done this for many years of my career and across a few schools, what tends to happen is that a vast amount of time is wasted on paperwork only for the child to be assessed at whatever level the teacher knows to be roughly correct based on their in-class observations and the child's performance in tests. In other words, this exercise in evidence-gathering is pointless, wasting time that teachers could spend planning better lessons or ensuring they maintain a sustainable work–life balance. Far too much 'assessment' has been devised and undertaken as a means of demonstrating diligence to visitors, with scant attention paid to whether the information gained is useful or remotely worth the effort. It sounds obvious, but assessment must have a purpose, and the time spent on it should be commensurate to the utility of the insight it provides and the changes in teaching that can be made as a result. In short, assessment should be formative, not performative.

—————————— Questions for professional discussion ——————————

- If you were a teacher taking on a new class, what information would you want to be given by the previous teacher in order to inform your teaching of reading?
- How well does this information tally with the reading assessments undertaken at your school(s)?

—————————— Retrieval quiz ——————————

1 In fluency assessments, what does WCPM stand for?
2 What other element of fluency should be assessed by the teacher?
3 What are the potential advantages and disadvantages of understanding a child's reading ability in terms of a reading age?

Further reading

- Christodoulou, D. (2017). *Making Good Progress? The Future of Assessment for Learning*. Oxford: Oxford University Press.

19

INTERVENTION

The most important, if somewhat trite, point to make about any reading intervention is this: it is always better to avoid the need for intervention. The best support for struggling readers is preventative rather than remedial.[1] It is sadly the case that readers who get off to a poor start often struggle to catch up.[2] Consequently, early reading instruction, phonics in particular, should contain within it systematic support for those that struggle, which helps *before* they fall behind. Nevertheless, even high-quality reading instruction may still not allow *all* children to learn to read at a pace that allows them to 'keep up' with the rest of their class (or, more accurately, keep up with the age-related expectations defined by authorities). In this case, reading intervention may be necessary.

Before any intervention takes place, it is essential that the area of reading difficulty is assessed and understood. Where possible, children that require support in various areas of reading should get concurrent support that recognises this. *If* the area of greatest need isn't obvious from informal teacher assessment, Figure 19.1 shows a simple flowchart that gives a very basic idea of how to prioritise intervention.

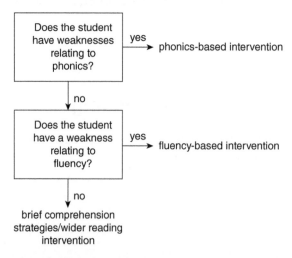

Figure 19.1 Flowchart that gives an idea of how to prioritise intervention

The majority of reading interventions that take place will require some form of phonics instruction. Evidence suggests that interventions that match the key phonics skills discussed in Chapter 4 are most effective: systematic phonics teaching with phoneme manipulation (blending, segmenting, phoneme replacement and phoneme deletion) and opportunities to practise using these skills while reading.[3] Naturally, any phonics teaching should align with the phonics programme taught across the school.

Where children show no weaknesses relating to phonics, then fluency interventions may be required. (The need for this will be apparent from fluency assessments; see Chapter 5.) Fluency practice can be employed as an intervention whereby children undertake repeated oral reading of a short, challenging text (around 1–2 minutes of reading) until they can read the text fluently. This continues, with the child's fluency with new texts monitored (in terms of WCPM and prosody, of course) as a way to assess the success of the intervention.

Where children's reading difficulties relate to neither phonics nor fluency, then a brief comprehension intervention may be beneficial. (Poor scores on standardised reading assessments despite average or above reading fluency would be an indication of the need for such an intervention.) Here, intervention should first involve comprehension strategies – specifically comprehension monitoring via self-questioning (including summarising and visualising) – and practice with local cohesion inferences relating to pronouns and connectives. As with all reading, this should take place using texts chosen to build the student's knowledge of the world. The majority of time spent in interventions relating directly to reading comprehension should be spent reading new text.

Whenever intervention is undertaken, the adult involved – be they a teacher or a member of support staff – must understand what is to be done and the rationale behind it. This will require school-wide training and ongoing discussions between all of the adults responsible for the reading development of the child in question.

In a nutshell …

- Try to avoid interventions wherever possible through systematic attempts to help all students 'keep up' with the learning of the rest of the class.
- Base interventions on assessments. Prioritise phonics; if this is not weak, prioritise fluency; if children's decoding is relatively fluent, then consider interventions relating to comprehension where the main component is the supervised reading with lots of text.

Other implications for the classroom

It is common practice in many schools for children who are struggling in an area deemed key – often reading, writing or mathematics – to undertake small-group interventions outside the classroom. These often take place while subjects such as geography or science are being taught, presumably as these subjects are deemed less essential. However, as we have seen (in Chapter 12), the understanding of the world which children gain in lessons such as geography or science contributes to their ability to read. This means that we need to be cautious when it comes to depriving children of aspects of the curriculum in order to undertake intervention teaching. While certain aspects of a child's learning such as phonics or basic numeracy may indeed take precedence for a time, we need to recognise that there are associated costs in terms of reading comprehension and consequently we need to be cautious in our use of out-of-class interventions.

The search for accountability in schools – frequently an attempt to measure the unmeasurable – often means that the choice and extent of interventions are not decided upon by the teacher alone. Meetings take place where two things tend to happen: several people become more informed on the needs of children who need support, and measurable targets are set for the proposed interventions. The former is definitely a good thing; the latter seems sensible enough, but often has unintended consequences. Useful interventions are sometimes ignored as they don't naturally offer measurable outcomes. For example, transforming a child's enthusiasm for reading through five minutes of one-to-one support per day is likely to pay dividends in the long term, but might provide no measurable outcome in the short term. In exceptional circumstances, regular, detailed intervention plans can become an unnecessary administrative burden, more of a box-ticking exercise than a genuine attempt to support the child in the most productive way possible. The target of every school should be to maximise the outcomes for the children while keeping paperwork for teachers to a reasonable minimum. This sometimes means being flexible on measurable outcomes and showing some faith in the judgement of teachers, something supported by opportunities for professional development.

--------------- Questions for professional discussions ---------------

- To what extent are interventions in your school(s) considered from a research-informed perspective?
- Are the trade-offs between targeted support and curriculum deprivation part of the discussion around interventions in your school(s)? To what extent do you think they should be?

--------------- Retrieval quiz ---------------

1 What must be done before a reading intervention is considered for a child?
2 What might be the indicators that suggest that a child should be considered for a reading intervention that specifically targets comprehension (rather than phonics or fluency)?

Further reading

- Kilpatrick, D. A., Joshi, R. M. and Wagner, R. K. (2019). *Reading Development and Difficulties*. Cham: Springer International Publishing.

References

1   National Reading Panel (US), National Institute of Child Health, Human Development (US), National Reading Excellence Initiative, National Institute for Literacy (US), United States. Public Health Service, & United States Department of Health (2000). *Report of the National Reading Panel: Teaching children to read: An evidence-based assessment of the scientific research literature on reading and its implications for reading instruction: Reports of the subgroups*. National Institute of Child Health and Human Development, National Institutes of Health.

2   Francis, D. J., Shaywitz, S. E., Stuebing, K. K., Shaywitz, B. A. and Fletcher, J. M. (1996). Developmental lag versus deficit models of reading disability: A longitudinal, individual growth curves analysis. *Journal of Educational Psychology*, 88(1), 3; Torgesen, J. K. and Burgess, S. R. (1998). Consistency of reading-related phonological processes throughout early childhood: Evidence from longitudinal-correlational and instructional studies. In Metsala, J. L. and Ehri, L. C. (eds), *Word Recognition in Beginning Literacy*. Mahwah, NJ: Lawrence Erlbaum Associates, 161–188.

3   Moats, L. (2019). Phonics and spelling: Learning the structure of language at the word level. In Kilpatrick, D. A., Joshi, R. M. and Wagner, R. K. (eds), *Reading Development and Difficulties*. Cham: Springer International Publishing, 39–62; Alexander, A. W., Andersen, H. G., Heilman, P. C., Voeller, K. K. and Torgesen, J. K. (1991). Phonological awareness training and remediation of analytic decoding deficits in a group of severe dyslexics. *Annals of Dyslexia*, 41(1), 193–206.

Part VI

The Reading Diet

20

THE CURRENT SITUATION

Picture a classroom of 10-year-old children. Their teacher knows that the class need to be able to answer 'inference questions' to get good marks in their end-of-year assessment. Consequently, the teacher decides that the best way to achieve this is to directly focus on how to answer such questions. (The school's reading coordinator – with one eye on end-of-school assessments – advocates this way of teaching.) In a standard reading session, the teacher gets the children to read for a few minutes before briefly discussing the text. The rest of the lesson is spent modelling how to answer inference questions and then getting children to try this independently. (The teacher is acting under the belief that inference is a generic, transferable skill.)

While children may well learn a little from this sort of lesson, the teaching is likely to be inefficient, at best. Yes, the new vocabulary encountered and the orthographic mapping supported in the first few minutes may well be useful, but the teacher's subsequent attempts to develop 'inference skills' are likely to be a poor use of time. The majority of the lesson is taken up by teaching that doesn't equate to much more than test practice. Even through the cynical lens of boosting outcomes, the gains are limited, with rapidly diminishing returns. Sadly, such teaching is common, though not universal, of course. Too much time is spent trying to teach skills that cannot be directly taught, using methods that are reverse-engineered from end-of-school assessments. It is the result of schools assuming that the product of reading comprehension (in formal assessment terms, at least) needs to match the method of developing it. It is akin to thinking that the way to make a plant taller is to pull it upwards rather than recognising the things that contribute to its growth and consistently supplying these. In other words, inefficient teaching of reading is often the result of a fundamental misunderstanding about the nature of reading comprehension, the components that constitute it and how these components can be developed.

Beyond teaching that is reverse-engineered from assessments, the other weakness commonly seen in the teaching of reading is the result of attempts at differentiation. Children learn to read at different rates and naturally will have different reading abilities at any given moment. The most common attempted solution to this problem involves sorting groups of children by current reading ability and having them read differently levelled texts. The upshot of this is that teachers have two options:

1   Give a different lesson to several groups of children, often called 'guided reading', in which at any given moment the majority of children are doing reading-related activities while entirely unsupported.
2   Move between groups of children, teaching them one group at a time, and then ask questions of the entire class that are so vague that they can apply to whatever text they happen to be reading (e.g. What is your favourite part of the text? What do the characters feel on the page you have read?)

Both of these options are inadvisable. In the first, children who cannot read fluently spend their time embedding this dysfluency. In the second, worthwhile discussion of the texts is limited to the brief moments where children are directly supervised. Thankfully, such methods can be avoided entirely. When it comes to text difficulty, there is no credible evidence supporting the practice of teaching children at *'their reading level'*.[1] Even the idea that working with more challenging texts will demotivate children has no basis in evidence.[2] All children learn at least equally well with a text that is challenging – though obviously to different degrees – for the entire class.[3] Teaching the whole class at once is a sensible default, though adaptations should be made using professional judgement to suit unique circumstances, including, where necessary, the teaching of phonics or fluency to small groups of children who are struggling relative to their peers. (Readers that particularly struggle often benefit from being exposed to the text or having extra reading time before a reading session.) The teaching methods that I will advocate through the rest of this book will be ones that involve an entire class reading the same text together. These methods will also focus on developing the different aspects that constitute skilled reading, rather than the generic comprehension skills that end-of-school assessments purport to measure.

In a nutshell ...

- Understand the different components of skilled reading. Teach these consistently and reading comprehension will develop. There is no shortcut, and methods that are reverse-engineered from end-of-school assessments are of very limited utility.
- Hearing children read one-to-one or in small groups can work, but it is a hopelessly inefficient way to organise reading instruction that is aimed at a whole class of students. Use methods that involve the whole class reading the same text as the default, and make necessary adaptations to allow this.

Further reading

- Shanahan, T. (2014). Should we teach students at their reading levels. *Reading Today*, 32(2), 14–15.
- *The Teachwell Blog.* www.teach-well.com.

References

1 Shanahan, T. (2014). Should we teach students at their reading levels. *Reading Today*, 32(2), 14–15; Vaites, K. (2019). *Leveled Reading Groups Don't Work – Why Aren't We Talking About It?* Eduvaites, 2 November. Available at: https://eduvaites.org/2019/11/02/leveled-reading-groups-dont-work-why-arent-we-talking-about-it/ (accessed 7 January 2021); Shanahan, T. (2020). *Teaching with Complex Text – Haven't You Heard of the ZPD?* Shanahan on Literacy, 22 August. Available at: https://shanahanonliteracy.com/blog/teaching-with-complex-text-havent-you-ever-heard-of-the-zpd (accessed 7 January 2021).

2 Gambrell, L. B., Wilson, R. M. and Gantt, W. N. (1981). Classroom observations of task-attending behaviors of good and poor readers. *Journal of Educational Research*, 74, 400–404; Fulmer, S. M. and Tulis, M. (2013). Changes in interest and affect during a difficult reading task: Relationships with perceived difficulty and reading fluency. *Learning and Instruction*, 27, 11–20.

3 Brown, L. T., Mohr, K. A., Wilcox, B. R. and Barrett, T. S. (2018). The effects of dyad reading and text difficulty on third-graders' reading achievement. *The Journal of Educational Research*, 111(5), 541–553.

21

FINDING A BALANCE

While there has been lots of research conducted into the aspects of reading instruction that have shown themselves to be relatively beneficial, there is little that relates to the balance required between these different aspects. For example, we know that repeated oral reading supports the development of fluency, but how much of this should a class undertake? And is this the same in Year 2 and Year 6? We know that the process of orthographic mapping implies that children decoding *lots* of text is essential to reading instruction, but exactly how do we achieve this? It can be tempting to think that the current science of reading alone provides answers to these questions, but it simply does not. What the research into reading *does* provide is the basis through which we can make informed decisions. Inevitably, though, these decisions will require judgement and experience. During my teaching career, I have at some point or other taught every age group between the ages of 4 and 11 years old. However, someone with several times this amount of teaching experience would still not be infallible. It is important to remember that the vast body of research into reading provides us only with best bets for nudging children's odds of success in the right direction. Nevertheless, I am convinced that teaching reading in a way that is informed by experience *and* that coheres with the available evidence is the best choice for the children we teach. This being the case, the rest of this book will detail my interpretation of the reading research based on my teaching experience and on countless discussions with fellow educators.

There are ways of thinking about reading instruction that allow us to best divide our time between the different essential aspects of reading. To allow discussion of the different aspects of reading instruction I will use the following labels for different aspects of teaching reading:

- Phonics instruction
- Fluency practice
- Extended reading

- Close reading
- Shared reading
- Vocabulary instruction
- Comprehension strategy instruction.

Phonics instruction

As discussed in Chapter 4, phonics instruction focuses on the explicit teaching of sound–spelling correspondences and phonemic awareness. It makes up a significant proportion of the reading instruction undertaken during children's first years at school.

The planning of phonics instruction must align with the school's phonics programme. Where possible, the planning of phonics should be discussed with colleagues to ensure that the learning time is being used optimally.

Fluency practice

As discussed in Chapter 5, fluency practice focuses on developing fluency through repeated oral reading of a short text or extract. The text needs to be long enough for children to not be able to memorise the entire thing, around 1–1.5 minutes of reading time. It should also be of a difficulty so that almost no child in the class can quite read the text fluently first time without modelling from the teacher.[1] A rough rule of thumb is that around 10% of the words in the text should be particularly for children to decode independently; choosing such texts becomes much easier as your knowledge of a class increases. In the lessons, the teacher reads the text aloud, modelling fluent reading. Any unfamiliar vocabulary and concepts should ideally be discussed during this model read, though this can also be done before or after the model read where the teacher deems it necessary. The teacher should discuss any reading goals that are especially relevant to the class or the text type, making explicit the mixture of fluency and comprehension that is to be achieved after repeated readings of the text. (When fluency practice is first introduced to a class, this goal-setting may even include an exaggeratedly monotonous or stilted reading of the text, followed by an ideal model read so that children can more clearly grasp what they are aiming for.) The class, who are sat in mixed-ability pairs, then attempt to read the text aloud to their partner. To ensure that both children are involved, the non-reading partner should track the line that is being read using a ruler. Once one partner has read the text, the partners switch roles. (Alternatively, the children can take it in turns to read a sentence as they progress down the text, switching who goes first on each read.) The idea is that every child will read the text aloud at least three times, aiming for greater fluency each time. Their partner is available to support, and the teacher can move around the room briefly hearing different reading pairs and pausing the class to model a particular word or sentence when required. The teacher should also give feedback that helps each student to be a better reading partner, for example by modelling how to ask for a sentence to be repeated or how to sensitively correct a decoding error. It is essential that children recognise that – while they may be practising their reading fluency – the main reason for their reading is to learn the interesting things that are contained within the text itself. Thus, all fluency practice should be accompanied by discussion of the text's contents, perhaps including questions for children to discuss and answer. Nevertheless, the majority of time spent undertaking fluency practice should be spent on repeated oral reading. The session may finish with a selected student or two reading the text aloud. This adds an extra sense of purpose to the fluency practice. (The selection of students to 'perform' the text should be undertaken sensitively as to not apply undue pressure to those who may be reluctant to read in front of an entire class. With support over time, even the most nervous of readers begins to relish the opportunity to read aloud if the teacher shows that the performance is very low stakes. Consistently avoiding praise for success in this situation can serve to remove any pressure that children might feel.)

Fluency practice is most important when children are first learning to use their decoding skills, and at this point it should constitute a significant proportion of their weekly reading time. As children's reading fluency increases, the amount of fluency practice should decrease.

The planning of a fluency practice session involves the following steps:

1 Select an appropriate text.
2 Identify new concepts and vocabulary in the text and consider explanations, preparing pictures where necessary.
3 Consider how to support children who may struggle to read the text at all; they may be supported by a stronger peer or another adult in the room; they may benefit from exposure to the text before the lesson.

Extended reading

Extended reading involves prolonged engagement with a longer text or extract and thus focuses on the development of fluency, word knowledge, background knowledge and text knowledge through exposure to text. There are effectively four different ways to undertake such reading, depending on the current reading abilities of the class:

1 The teacher reads to the class as they follow the text, keeping pace with a ruler. Accountability can be ensured by the teacher pausing and asking the class to say the next word in the text in unison.
2 Children, selected by the teacher, take it in turns to read a few sentences aloud while the rest of the class keep pace with a ruler. The teacher also occasionally takes a turn

to model fluent reading. Accountability can be ensured by quick transitions between readers and by the teacher pausing and asking the class to say the next word in the text in unison when it is the teacher's turn to read.[2]

3   Children read silently in short bursts, the length of which are carefully managed by the teacher. At first, the amount of reading to be done is very short to minimise the issues caused by the children's different reading speeds, and over time as the children's ability develops, the amount of reading in each burst is increased.[3]

4   Children read for extended periods in silence from a shared text. Due to differences in reading speeds, questions are prepared for early finishers to ensure that they have actually read the text and have attempted to comprehend its meaning.

Classes of children should be moved on to the next stage of extended reading as soon as they are ready for it. Extended reading methods (1) and (2) in particular should only be used where an inability to decode means that silent reading will only result in consolidating dysfluency. In my experience, children can begin the transition to short bursts of silent reading, followed by quick discussion and questions from a teacher, at the age of 7–8 years.

Extended reading should be accompanied by discussion and related questions for children to answer to probe their understanding of the text. Most of the time, this discussion should take place at key points in the text, meaning that planning entails teachers dissecting a text and picking key moments where children may need to clarify, summarise or explore the meaning in the text. Any unfamiliar vocabulary and concepts should ideally be discussed as they are encountered in the text, though this can also be done before the reading begins where the teacher deems it necessary. Children may be required to write answers to questions to reinforce what they have learned. This is a good way for the teacher to assess whether something has been understood, but it is the reading itself and the related discussion that will most advance children's ability to read. In some cases, the children may read a text for a significant period of time followed by discussion and answering questions. While this may be a valuable assessment opportunity, discussion of a text is best undertaken at key moments as the text is read. If in doubt, aim for roughly two-thirds of the lesson to comprise reading and one-third of the lesson to comprise discussion.

The planning of an extended reading session involves the following steps:

1   Select an appropriate text.
2   Identify new concepts and vocabulary in the text and consider explanations, preparing pictures where necessary.
3   Identify key stopping points in the text where children will clarify, summarise or explore the meaning of the text.
4   Plan the questions that will be asked at these stopping points, considering how to further the discussion based on predicted answers from children; also consider whether the children will respond to these questions independently, after partner discussions or in writing. (Responses in writing would likely be rarer. There is no need for children to spend lots of time writing in a reading session.)

Close reading

Close reading involves the sustained, detailed analysis of a short text or extract and thus focuses on the development of word knowledge, background knowledge and text knowledge through deep discussion.[4] Consequently, close reading involves repeated reading of a text whereby the first read gives an overall sense of the text, and subsequent reads involve the discussion of particular themes, vocabulary choices, literary devices, plot points or anything else worthy of focus. For example, this may involve jumping through a text looking for a writer's use of metaphors, or it might involve looking at a paragraph line-by-line to see how tension is built by an author. As with the other reading sessions, any unfamiliar vocabulary and concepts should ideally be discussed as they are encountered in the text, though this can also be done before the reading begins where the teacher deems it necessary.

Close reading will naturally involve rich discussion of the text at hand, and it may also involve children answering questions independently in writing. However – and excuse my labouring this point – it is the reading itself and the related discussion that will most advance children's ability to read.

Although children can begin deeply engaging with a text as soon as they can decode with a little fluency, close reading sessions become more suitable – and more productive – as children's reading develops. If in doubt aim for roughly one-third of the lesson to comprise reading and two-thirds of the lesson to comprise discussion.

The planning of a close reading session involves the following steps:

1   Select an appropriate text.
2   Identify new concepts and vocabulary in the text and consider explanations, preparing pictures where necessary.
3   Identify key stopping points in the text where children will clarify, summarise or explore the meaning of the text.
4   Plan the questions that will be asked at these stopping points, considering how to further the discussion based on anticipated answers from children; also consider whether the children will respond to these questions independently, following partner discussions or in writing. (Responses in writing would likely be rarer. There is no need for children to spend lots of time writing in a reading session.)
5   Consider what aspects of a text will be focused upon during different reads of the text (e.g. first read establishes meaning; second read focuses on the author's use of rhetorical questions; etc.).

Shared reading

Shared reading involves a teacher reading aloud to children with brief discussion of the text and as a result focuses on the development of listening comprehension, word knowledge, background knowledge and reading enjoyment. The child's central role in this type of reading is to listen carefully, to try to derive meaning from what they hear and to enjoy the process of doing both.

Vocabulary instruction

Children will learn a great deal of vocabulary in the reading sessions outlined above. If tier two vocabulary and root words are deeply embedded in your wider curriculum with opportunities for retrieval, standalone vocabulary sessions may well be unnecessary. Where this is not possible, however, discrete vocabulary instruction guarantees that valuable words that are currently beyond the scope of your school's curriculum are still understood by children. Short bursts of instruction, perhaps just 5–10 minutes per day, can support vocabulary development under these circumstances. This can be undertaken by referring to a timetable for the introduction of tier two vocabulary and Latin and Greek root words (see Appendix C for an example timetable) in which each day a tier two word or root word is introduced or revised. The children then engage with the words in question, creating sentences orally or in writing, and the teacher can use low-stakes quizzes to promote memory of these. While learning any vocabulary outside of an immediately applicable context isn't ideal, in my experience a context for the vocabulary will tend to find you. Show children that 'cent' relates to 'one hundred', and they will soon be pointing out words like 'centipede', 'centimetre' and 'century' in the language they hear and the texts they read.

Formal instruction of tier two vocabulary and Latin and Greek root words tends to work best when children are a little older, around the age of 7–8 years. However, there is of course no harm in informally pointing out such vocabulary before this formal teaching begins.

The planning of a discrete vocabulary session involves the following steps:

1 Identify the tier two word or Latin/Greek root word that will be the focus of the session.
2 Consider the child-friendly explanation of the word that will be shared and the different contexts that the word will be shown in, preparing pictures where necessary.
3 Prepare a task that ensures the class actively use the word in speech or writing.
4 Consider how the word will be retrieved at a later date, either in a subsequent vocabulary session or across the rest of the curriculum.

Comprehension strategy instruction

As discussed in Chapters 8 and 9, there is strong evidence to suggest that the brief teaching of specific comprehension strategies is beneficial. In particular, explicit teaching of cohesive devices (e.g. pronouns and connectives) and comprehension monitoring via self-questioning (including summarising and visualising) can be taught to children with positive impacts on reading comprehension outcomes.[5]

There are two ways to teach comprehension strategies. *The first way* is to dedicate some reading sessions each year to the explicit teaching of these strategies. This involves explaining and clearly modelling a strategy, scaffolding children's use of the strategy and then ensuring that children can use the strategy independently. For example, children could read a short story, and the teacher could then model summarising the story, explaining his or her thought processes along the way. The children would then be supported to summarise a different story, perhaps choosing from different summaries and discussing which works best and why. Then, the children would attempt to summarise a story independently. This process is then repeated for two or three different text types, with the similarities and differences between the summaries discussed. Finally, this summarising strategy is embedded in the reading teaching that follows. This method best aligns with how comprehension strategy instruction is described in the applied research that has been conducted on the subject.

The second way to teach comprehension strategies is to integrate them into extended reading and close reading sessions. This involves using the discussion within these sessions to model and practise self-questioning (including visualising and summarising) and the use of cohesive devices, always relating these to the content of the chosen text. The upside to this approach is that it provides a more natural way to include comprehension strategies into reading lessons. The downside is that the teacher needs to take great care to ensure that these comprehension strategies do not become the central component of reading lessons. A couple of minutes each lesson modelling, practising and reinforcing these metacognitive strategies as an organic part of reading lessons should be plenty. However, planning for the modelling and gradual increase in children's independent use of these strategies within extended reading and close reading sessions is certainly the more challenging approach for teachers to plan and undertake. Which approach you choose will depend on your own circumstances and experience.

Comprehension strategies are best taught to children aged 7–11 years as the related research mostly relates to children of this age or older. It is also worth reiterating that reading experts generally advocate relatively brief teaching of these strategies. Comprehension strategy instruction is like vitamin supplements. They are a useful part of the reading diet, but they are only needed in small doses. Once children have been taught to decode, the majority of reading instruction should involve the reading and discussing of text.

The reading diet

So, how might this all look in practice? I do not want you to think that what follows is the *only* way to combine the essential aspects of reading instruction. It very much reflects my personal synthesis of the reading research. As such, it is perfectly plausible that someone would grasp the reading research described in the first five parts of this book and create a very different – and equally sensible – overview of reading across a school.

Think of the set of timetables outlined below as just one example of how to ensure that children receive a balanced reading diet.

Reception

Table 21.1 Example timetable for Reception

Monday	Tuesday	Wednesday	Thursday	Friday
		phonics		
		(30–45 mins daily)		
		shared reading		
		(20 mins daily)		

Note in particular:

1   The shared reading should occasionally involve the text being visible on screen and the words being pointed to one at a time as a teacher reads slightly below their normal pace. This is useful in developing children's concept of word and their understanding of print conventions (as discussed in Chapter 4).
2   The time spent on phonics or shared reading may be broken up into shorter chunks through the school day, depending on the needs of the individual class. Also, the rest of the school day will naturally involve lots of rich talk, something that will support reading (and every other aspect of learning).
3   As frequently as classroom arrangements allow, each child should also read to an adult on a one-to-one basis.

Year 1

Table 21.2 Example timetable for Year 1

Monday	Tuesday	Wednesday	Thursday	Friday
		phonics		
		(30–45 mins daily)		
		shared reading		
		(20 mins daily)		

Note in particular:

1   Depending on the availability of resources, phonically controlled books may also be read by children in the classroom as part of the daily phonics session. This can be done under a visualiser or, ideally, with books read by pairs of children as a transition into the fluency practice in Year 2 and beyond.
2   There will also inevitably be some instruction relating to early writing. Activities relating to transcription and use of the sound–spelling correspondences that children have learned will further support reading.
3   As frequently as classroom arrangements allow, each child should also read to an adult on a one-to-one basis.

Year 2

Table 21.3 Example timetable for Year 2

Monday	Tuesday	Wednesday	Thursday	Friday
phonics (30–45 mins daily)				
fluency practice (30 mins)	extended reading (30 mins)	fluency practice (30 mins)	extended reading (30 mins)	fluency practice (30 mins)
shared reading (20 mins daily)				

Year 3

Table 21.4 Example timetable for Year 3

Monday	Tuesday	Wednesday	Thursday	Friday
vocabulary instruction (10 mins daily – see timetable in Appendix C)				
phonics/spelling (30 mins daily)				
fluency practice (30 mins)	extended reading (30 mins)	fluency practice (30 mins)	extended reading (30 mins)	close reading (30 mins)
shared reading (20 mins daily)				

Note in particular:

1 Comprehension strategy instruction can be integrated into extended reading and close reading sessions. Alternatively, comprehension strategy instruction in summarising should take place instead of extended reading, close reading and fluency practice for the *first two weeks of the school year* and then be embedded into teaching thereafter.
2 Discrete vocabulary instruction as shown on the timetable will be unnecessary if the tier two vocabulary and root words are deeply embedded within the wider curriculum.

Year 4

Table 21.5 Example timetable for Year 4

Monday	Tuesday	Wednesday	Thursday	Friday
vocabulary instruction (10 mins daily – see timetable in Appendix C)				
phonics/spelling (30 mins daily)				
fluency practice (30 mins)	extended reading (30 mins)	fluency practice (30 mins)	extended reading (30 mins)	close reading (30 mins)
shared reading (20 mins daily)				

Note in particular:

1   Comprehension strategy instruction can be integrated into extended reading and close reading sessions. Alternatively, comprehension strategy instruction in the use of anaphora (e.g. pronouns) and connectives should take place instead of fluency practice, extended reading and close reading for the *first two weeks of the school year* and then be embedded into teaching thereafter.
2   Discrete vocabulary instruction as shown on the timetable will be unnecessary if the tier two vocabulary and root words are deeply embedded within the wider curriculum.

Year 5

Table 21.6   Example timetable for Year 5

Monday	Tuesday	Wednesday	Thursday	Friday
vocabulary instruction				
(10 mins daily – see timetable in Appendix C)				
phonics/spelling				
(30 mins daily)				
extended reading	close reading	fluency practice	extended reading	close reading
(30 mins)	(30 mins)	(30 mins)	(30 mins)	(30 mins)
shared reading				
(20 mins daily)				

Note in particular:

1   Comprehension strategy instruction can be integrated into extended reading and close reading sessions. Alternatively, comprehension strategy instruction in self-questioning should take place instead of extended reading, close reading and fluency practice for the *first two weeks of the school year* and then be embedded into teaching thereafter.
2   Discrete vocabulary instruction as shown on the timetable will be unnecessary if the tier two vocabulary and root words are deeply embedded within the wider curriculum.

Year 6

Table 21.7   Example timetable for Year 6

Monday	Tuesday	Wednesday	Thursday	Friday
vocabulary instruction				
(10 mins daily – see timetable in Appendix C)				
phonics/spelling				
(30 mins daily)				
extended reading	close reading	extended reading	close reading	extended reading
(30 mins)	(30 mins)	(30 mins)	(30 mins)	(30 mins)
shared reading				
(20 mins daily)				

Note in particular:

1   Comprehension strategy instruction can be integrated into extended reading and close reading sessions. Alternatively, comprehension strategy instruction that revises the strategies introduced in Years 3–5 should take place instead of extended reading, close reading and fluency practice for *the first two weeks of the school year* and then be embedded into teaching thereafter.
2   Discrete vocabulary instruction as shown on the timetable will be unnecessary if the tier two vocabulary and root words are deeply embedded within the wider curriculum.
3   The teaching of writing throughout Years 1–6 should include an understanding of text structure, ideally using text maps of specific texts where appropriate and generalising beyond these to an understanding of genre and conventions.

Naturally, the timetables suggested above would need to be adapted to meet the needs of children in a given class. For example, if a Year 6 class contained a significant number of children whose reading fluency, following assessment, was deemed an issue, then fluency practice sessions could still be incorporated as part of the weekly reading instruction. It is important to understand what the different reading sessions support, so that the right balance can be found for a given class. Equally, a reading timetable might be organised so that each type of reading (close reading, fluency practice, etc.) is included in a single session each day in a correct balance for the class in question. Nevertheless, while I think that this may well be possible, my personal experience has been that the different aspects of reading can be far more easily balanced by teaching them as separate sessions.

The fallacy of linear progression

Unavoidably, the contents of a book must be presented in a linear order. To a large extent, this book presents the elements of reading in an order which best matches their development. It is true to say that comprehension depends on reading fluency, which itself depends on decoding, which in turn depends on children's phonemic awareness. It is easy to get the impression from this order that the *teaching* of each stage must inevitably progress in this linear fashion with each element waiting for the previous element to be sufficiently consolidated before learning can commence. Such an impression, however, would be wrong.[6] While a view of progression comprising one-at-a-time steps offers a certain logical neatness, it does not tally with how learning to read actually takes place most effectively. For example, the development of phonemic awareness, which at first glance seems like pre-requisite knowledge for learning to decode, actually develops most efficiently in tandem with decoding skills.[7] The same is true of other areas of reading development: while reading fluency is necessary for reading comprehension, improving a child's comprehension of language supports the development of their reading fluency. Equally, a broad, deep vocabulary is crucial for reading comprehension, but comprehending what one reads also leads to gains in vocabulary. In brief, the apparent stages of learning to read are not best learned one at a time. There is a reciprocal relationship between them, and they should be taught together. This is reflected in the suggested reading timetables above.

———————————————————— In a nutshell … ————————————————

- Balance the different aspects of reading instruction based on where children are in their journey to skilled reading.
- Understand that *all* aspects of reading are being developed at the same time, but that certain aspects will require greater emphasis at key points (e.g. phonics for early readers; fluency practice as decoding begins to develop).

Further reading

- Lemov, D., Driggs, C. and Woolway, E. (2016). *Reading Reconsidered: A Practical Guide to Rigorous Literacy Instruction.* San Francisco, CA: Jossey-Bass.

References

1 Shanahan, T. (2017). *How to Teach Fluency So It Takes.* Shanahan on Literacy, 17 September. Available at: https://shanahanonliteracy.com/blog/how-to-teach-fluency-so-that-it-takes (accessed 7 January 2021).
2 Lemov, D., Driggs, C. and Woolway, E. (2016). *Reading Reconsidered: A Practical Guide to Rigorous Literacy Instruction.* San Francisco, CA: Jossey-Bass.
3 Shanahan, T. (2020). *Silent Reading Comprehension Is Worth Teaching Even at a Distance.* Shanahan on Literacy, 15 August. Available at: https://shanahanonliteracy.com/blog/silent-reading-comprehension-is-worth-teaching-even-at-a-distance (accessed 7 January 2021).
4 Liben, M. (2020). Close reading, textual evidence, and source analysis. In Patterson, J. (ed.), *The SAT® Suite and Classroom Practice: English Language Arts/Literacy.* New York: College Board, 31–51.
5 Oakhill, J., Cain, K. and Elbro, C. (2014). *Understanding and Teaching Reading Comprehension: A Handbook.* London: Routledge.
6 Shanahan (2020).

7   Lonigan, C. J. and Shanahan, T. (2009). *Developing Early Literacy: Report of the National Early Literacy Panel. Executive Summary. A Scientific Synthesis of Early Literacy Development and Implications for Intervention*. Washington, DC: National Institute for Literacy; Perfetti, C. A., Beck, I., Bell, L. C. and Hughes, C. (1987). Phonemic knowledge and learning to read are reciprocal: A longitudinal study of first grade children. *Merrill-Palmer Quarterly*, 33(3), 283–319.

22

QUESTIONING AND DISCUSSION

Careful questioning and discussion have a unique capacity to provoke thought and support learning. They can be used before, during and after a text has been read, depending on the nature of the questions and the purpose of the reading session. Beyond phonics instruction, the central purpose for reading in every lesson should be the deriving of meaning from a worthwhile text. Even in a fluency practice session where fluency is a central goal, deriving meaning is still essential. Questioning and discussion are key to this.

As a rule, I would tend to use questioning and discussion in the following ways for the different sorts of reading sessions:

- Fluency practice – questioning and discussion mostly reserved for before and after repeated oral reading to allow focus on developing fluency.
- Extended reading – questioning throughout the session at key points determined by planning, including discussion of vocabulary and clarification of meaning; around one-third of the session spent discussing the text.
- Close reading – deep, prolonged questioning and discussion throughout the session; around two-thirds of the session spent discussing the text.
- Shared reading – brief discussion of vocabulary and meaning where necessary; enjoyment and flow of the text prioritised.
- Vocabulary instruction – questioning and discussion throughout the session.
- Comprehension strategy instruction – questioning and discussion throughout the session.

(The fractions used above are a *very* rough estimate, and individual sessions may vary greatly based on teachers' professional judgement. What is important to take away is the idea that extended reading sessions mostly involve reading text with some analysis; close reading sessions, in comparison, involve less time spent reading and more time spent on text analysis.)

Types of question

According to Lemov, Driggs and Woolway's (2016) *Reading Reconsidered,* questions asked in reading sessions can be productively thought of as serving two distinct purposes: establishing meaning and analysing meaning.[1] The former gives us a grasp of exactly what meaning is being expressed; the latter unpicks exactly how and why this expression of meaning works. The authors of *Reading Reconsidered* advocate using questions that consider a text at different levels and 'zooming in' and 'zooming out' between the word/phrase level and the paragraph or text level. They also advocate 'toggling' between questions that establish meaning and those that analyse meaning. Combining these ideas allows us to consider the sorts of questions that will establish and analyse meaning from the word level up to the text level (see Table 22.1).

Table 22.1 Establishing and analysing meaning

	Establishing meaning	Analysing meaning
Text level	summary e.g. Summarise the plot of this book in a brief paragraph. genre questions e.g. What kind of text is this? How can you tell?	thematic e.g. Why is _____ an appropriate/ unusual setting for this story? Is _____ a kind character? Explain your answer with evidence.
Paragraph/chapter level	summary e.g. Summarise this paragraph in a single sentence. evidence finder e.g. Find the evidence in this paragraph that shows that ...	purpose e.g. Why is this chapter a turning point in the story? Who is the most important character in this chapter? How is this paragraph different from the one before?
Sentence/line level	paraphrase e.g. Write this sentence again in different words.	sentence structure and punctuation e.g. Why is this word repeated? What does this ellipsis show? significance question e.g. What is this sentence showing? How does this sentence contrast with the rest of the paragraph?
Word/phrase level	anaphora e.g. What does 'it' refer to here? denotation e.g. What does _____ mean?	connotation e.g. What does _____ mean in this context? What might _____ suggest to the reader in this context? sensitivity analysis e.g. What is the effect on this sentence if we change/remove _____?

The questions in Table 22.1 are quite formal and abstract in nature. While we want children to be able to deal with questions in this form, it is often the case that they come to grasp the purpose of reading by having these questions re-focused on the author.[2] Compare Table 22.2 to Table 22.1.

Table 22.2 Establishing and analysing meaning with a focus on the author

	Establishing meaning	Analysing meaning
Text level	summary e.g. In a brief paragraph, summarise the plot that the author communicated in this book. genre questions e.g. What kind of text has the author tried to create? How can you tell?	thematic e.g. Why is _____ an appropriate/unusual setting for the author to have chosen for this story? Has the author written _____ as a kind character? Explain your answer with evidence.
Paragraph/ chapter level	summary e.g. Summarise what the author communicated in this paragraph in a single sentence. evidence finder e.g. Find the evidence provided by the author in this paragraph that shows that ...	purpose e.g. How did the author make this chapter a turning point in the story? Who did the author make the most important character in this chapter? How did the author make this paragraph different from the one before?
Sentence/line level	paraphrase e.g. Write this sentence again in different words from the ones chosen by the author.	sentence structure and punctuation e.g. Why did the author repeat this word? What did the author want this ellipsis to show? significance question e.g. What did the author want this sentence to show? How did the author contrast this sentence with the rest of the paragraph?
Word/phrase level	anaphora e.g. What does 'it' refer to here? denotation e.g. What did the author mean by _____?	connotation e.g. What did the author mean by _____ in this context? What might the author want _____ to suggest to the reader in this context? sensitivity analysis e.g. If we change/remove _____, how does this change the meaning of the sentence from the way the author intended?

Most of the questions in Table 22.2 remind children that reading is about the communication of meaning by a writer and the reconstruction of this meaning by the reader. In my experience, such questioning also has the potential to support children's understanding of writing. My preference is to use this kind of author-orientated questioning as the default while ensuring through practice that children are increasingly confident with the more impersonal questioning exemplified in Table 22.1. In some circumstances, however, a focus on the author can make questions harder to comprehend. In such cases, this difficulty can be avoided by breaking the question into multiple questions. For example, 'Why is _____ an appropriate setting for the author to have chosen for this story?' may be better worded as two questions: 'Why is this an appropriate setting for this story? Why do you think the author chose this setting?' Notice that these questions still bring us back to the author while scaffolding children's thinking and the related discussion.

The above types of questions are not an exhaustive list, and they are considerably weakened by their generic nature. High-quality questions should support children to understand *the specific text being read* and thus be intimately related to that text. (The authors of *Reading Reconsidered* describe such questions as 'text dependent' for precisely this reason.) Like so many other aspects of reading, effective questioning works by helping children to gradually accumulate understanding, one text at a time.

Part of the art of questioning and discussion in the classroom is knowing how and when to elicit further thinking from children, particularly after they have given an initial response to a question. The best discussion often comes when a teacher, depending on the response given, then invites a student to clarify ('What exactly do you mean by …?'), to justify ('Why do you think that …?'), to connect ('In what ways is this similar to/different from …?'), to hypothesise ('What might be the consequence of …?') or to reflect ('How did you decide …?').[3] The question stems in brackets are mere examples of the countless ways in which a teacher can stimulate further discussion from an initial response. It may seem obvious, but quality discussion depends on teachers genuinely listening to children's responses and guiding the discussion from there. Sometimes this will mean exploring avenues of enquiry that the teacher had not considered before the lesson; on other occasions it will mean guiding children back to a key point that is worthy of focus. There is no simple metric that I can give for how to find this balance. Nevertheless, I would recommend that, if at all possible, you film yourself guiding a discussion in reading. Observing these interactions away from the point of teaching is invaluable. Equally, discussing this aspect of your teaching with colleagues, especially those with more experience, is an excellent way to improve, as is observing other teachers. (When it comes to professional development, observing others is often far more beneficial than being observed.)

An important but tricky aspect of classroom discussion is ensuring that children are listening to one another and building on one another's responses. Developing this sort of classroom culture requires the teacher to consistently make it clear that every response – regardless of how unexpected or even misguided – is valued. Of course, where a student has drawn a plainly inaccurate conclusion – for example, mistaking the definition of a word – then this should be corrected, but the sensitivity of this correction and the appreciation for the initial response is crucial in what it shows to children about the importance of respectful dialogue. When classroom discussion becomes a truly collaborative experience, it has the potential to surprise, to invigorate and to sensitise young minds to the possibilities afforded by reading.

———————————————— In a nutshell … ————————————————

- Match the type of questions and discussion, and their timing, to the aims of the reading session.
- Use questioning and discussion to establish meaning and analyse meaning from the word level up to the text level.

Further reading

- James Durran Blog. https://jamesdurran.blog.
- Lemov, D., Driggs, C. and Woolway, E. (2016). *Reading Reconsidered: A Practical Guide to Rigorous Literacy Instruction*. San Francisco, CA: Jossey-Bass.

References

1   Lemov, D., Driggs, C. and Woolway, E. (2016). *Reading Reconsidered: A Practical Guide to Rigorous Literacy Instruction*. San Francisco, CA: Jossey-Bass.
2   Beck, I. L. and McKeown, M. G. (2002). Questioning the author: Making sense of social studies. *Educational Leadership*, 59(3), 44–47.
3   Durran, J. (2017). *Asking Real Questions in the Classroom*. James Durran Blog, 7 June. Available at: https://jamesdurran.blog/?s=asking+real+questions (accessed 7 January 2021).

23

CHOOSING TEXTS

At this stage, it should be apparent that the choice of texts made by teachers is hugely significant. Beyond the development of fluency through orthographic mapping, the key thing that children will learn while reading is vocabulary, background knowledge, sentence structure and text structure. Text choice allows teachers to carefully select the dots that will be applied to each child's pointillist picture of understanding.

The first thing that teachers should do is ensure that children are exposed to texts of suitable variety. This means a variety of subject matter, text types and underlying text structures (see Chapter 10). Ideally, children's reading should span the curriculum as a proxy for the breadth of human knowledge to which they are being introduced at school. In particular, studies have shown that informational texts are an excellent medium through which to develop the background knowledge of young children.[1] The extent to which informational texts are prevalent in later education also means that accustoming children to texts of this type is likely to be worthwhile.[2] As a rule, around half of the reading that children should undertake should be narrative fiction. The other half should be composed of poetry, drama, narrative non-fiction (e.g. biographies) and expository texts (e.g. factual reports, speeches, newspaper articles, advertisements, letters, etc). Variety is key.

The second thing that teachers should do is pitch the texts at or just beyond the current abilities of the more able readers in the class. As discussed earlier, there is no evidence that it is ineffective or demotivating for children to learn from texts that are considerably more challenging than they are used to. It is better to pitch a text high and provide support and scaffolding than to lower expectations through use of less-demanding texts.

The third thing teachers should do is consider the diversity of backgrounds and experiences that is reflected back at children when they read texts in reading lessons or when class novels are shared. Children have a right to feel like they are represented by the texts that they read and have read to them. This *does not* mean avoiding classic texts because they are not representative of the modern world. It *does* mean that thought should go into the breadth of texts that children encounter as they progress through school.

School leaders may decide to select a canon of reading that children will experience during their time at school. At its most ambitious, a canon may identify all the books that children will encounter from reception to Year 6, alongside all the poetry, biographies, information texts, etc. that they will read and that are linked to the school's wider curriculum. (Naturally, this requires a great deal of investment and organisation from a school to ensure that copies of the texts are available to be used.) Alternatively, a school's canon may just equate to a few key texts that children will experience during their journey through school. Either way, it is critical that the texts are chosen with due attention afforded to variety, pitch and the diversity of backgrounds and experiences represented within those texts.

──────────────────── In a nutshell … ────────────────────

- Teach children using a variety of text types with a variety of content that spans the curriculum (and beyond) and reflects the diversity of backgrounds and experiences of the school community and wider society.

References

1   Williams, J. P., Stafford, K. B., Lauer, K. D., Hall, K. M. and Pollini, S. (2009). Embedding reading comprehension training in content-area instruction. *Journal of Educational Psychology*, 101(1), 1–20.
2   Venezky, R. (2000). The origins of the present-day chasms between adult literacy needs and school literacy instruction. *Scientific Studies of Reading*, 4(1), 19–39.

24

AN ACTION PLAN FOR CLASSROOM TEACHERS

In this chapter, I will suggest a potential action plan for classroom teachers. This is not to imply that every aspect of the action plan should be tackled immediately. In many cases, the points on the action plan will relate to areas in which you are already confident. The idea is that this action plan can be used to identify and prioritise individual areas for improvement that can be developed one at a time.

For teachers of initial readers

- Understand the sound-to-print logic behind phonics and teach accordingly.
- Provide day-to-day support as a priority for those that have not grasped aspects of the initial code; on the rare occasions that children persistently struggle, ensure that your reading coordinator is aware of this.
- Ensure access to phonically controlled books while children are learning the initial/basic code of your school's phonics programme.
- Develop children's concept of word by occasionally allowing them to see the words being read aloud, indicated by a finger pointing at the words.

For all teachers

- Teach spelling using the logic behind English orthography from phonics.
- Assess the reading fluency of the children in your class at least twice a year.
- Teach reading fluency using repeated oral reading of short texts and extracts, and appreciate that dysfluency is often the underlying cause of poor comprehension.

- Prioritise quantitative aspects of reading to ensure extensive opportunities for orthographic mapping.
- Teach vocabulary by prioritising tier two words alongside instruction on morphology and etymology.
- Undertake reading sessions that explicitly prioritise the content of the text through questioning and discussion.
- Understand that reading comprehension can be thought of as the process of creating and updating a situation model that reflects the meaning of the text.
- Appreciate that children often struggle to make local cohesion inferences; accordingly, teach children about the function of pronouns (and other forms of anaphora) and connectives in reading sessions and writing sessions.
- Teach children the typical features and structures of different types of text in reading sessions and writing sessions.
- Teach strategies that guide children to monitor their own comprehension and to set an appropriate standard for coherence via self-questioning (including summarising and self-questioning); after modelling and scaffolding these strategies, support children's independent use of them. This can be achieved as brief standalone sessions or as an integral part of reading lessons.
- Understand how the different aspects of language comprehension – comprehension monitoring, background knowledge, vocabulary, inference and knowledge of text structures – are mutually supportive.
- Read aloud to children daily, briefly discussing new concepts and vocabulary in this context in a way that does not undermine the central aim of this time: enjoyment.
- Encourage children occasionally to try new types of books while allowing them freedom to make the final decision on what they want to read; these books should represent the diversity of your school and the wider community.
- Take opportunities to embed reading across the curriculum, including disciplinary reading for older students.
- Where necessary, consider interventions that specifically match the needs of individual children or a small group; where children have multiple reading difficulties prioritise phonics, then fluency, then comprehension strategies alongside the development of vocabulary, background knowledge, knowledge of sentence structure and knowledge of text structure.
- Understand the utility and limits of 'dyslexia' as a label of word-reading difficulties.

25

AN ACTION PLAN FOR READING COORDINATORS

In this chapter, I will suggest a potential action plan for reading coordinators. This is not to imply that every aspect of the action plan should be tackled immediately. In many cases, the points on the action plan will relate to areas in which you are already confident. The idea is that this action plan can be used to identify and prioritise individual areas for improvement that can be developed one at a time.

- Provide continuing professional development (CPD) opportunities to ensure all teaching staff understand the sound-to-print logic behind phonics and the essential vocabulary required to teach phonics systematically; prioritise this understanding with new teaching staff.
- Track the phonics attainment of children throughout the school and ensure that the teaching and, where necessary, systematic intervention matches this.
- Ensure that your school's phonically controlled books closely match the phonics programme used by your school; this should mean that children have the chance to regularly practise decoding from books containing familiar sound–spelling correspondences when they are first learning to decode.
- Ensure that the spelling progression across the school does not conflict with the logic behind English orthography from phonics.
- Provide CPD for all teaching staff on the administration of fluency assessments; using these assessments, track the fluency of all children across the school, starting at an appropriate age (usually aged 6–7 years).
- Provide CPD on effective fluency practice via repeated oral reading of challenging texts.
- Provide teachers with a systematic timetable for introducing and teaching well-chosen tier two vocabulary and Latin and Greek root words, ideally as a coherent part of the wider curriculum; ensure teachers understand morphology and that the discussion of morphology with children is appropriately consistent across the school.

- Keep track of the quantitative aspects of reading across the school; know roughly how many minutes per week children spend decoding in each year group.
- Provide CPD on close reading and extended reading sessions that explicitly prioritise the content of the text through questioning and discussion.
- Support teachers to teach strategies that guide children to monitor their own comprehension and to set an appropriate standard for coherence via self-questioning (including visualising and summarising); after modelling and scaffolding these strategies, support children's independent use of them. This can be structured as brief standalone sessions or as an integral part of reading lessons.
- Provide CPD to support teachers in understanding how the different aspects of language comprehension – comprehension monitoring, background knowledge, vocabulary, inference and knowledge of text structures – are mutually supportive.
- Ensure that the daily time allotted for teachers to read aloud to children is sacrosanct.
- Ensure children have access to a variety of high-quality fiction and non-fiction books; if your school employs a book-banding system to support children's choices and teachers' ability to recommend books, ensure that this does not prohibit children from choosing books that match their preference.
- Discuss with subject coordinators and curriculum leaders the embedding of reading into other aspects of the curriculum and the possibility of a disciplinary view of reading with older children.
- Where necessary, consider interventions that specifically match the needs of individual children or small groups; where children have multiple reading difficulties prioritise phonics, then fluency, then comprehension strategies alongside the development of vocabulary, background knowledge, knowledge of sentence structure and knowledge of text structure.
- Appreciate the utility and limits of 'dyslexia' as a label for word-reading difficulties, and ensure that your understanding of this is consistent with the person in charge of supporting children with additional learning needs in your school.

AFTERWORD

As I draw this book to a close, I would like to refer back to its recurring metaphor, that of pointillist painting. There are two important ways that the teaching of reading mirrors the creation of such art.

First, teaching reading comprehension is a meticulous process. It is the purposeful, gradual adding of dots to the canvas of children's understanding. Each word, each sentence and each paragraph is an opportunity to add further dots, and this is best achieved by focusing on the meaning of well-chosen texts, one by one. Effective reading instruction does not consist of the illusory broad brushstrokes of comprehension skills. There is no *generic* skill of inference making; in any lesson, we can only teach children about the *specific* inferences of a given text. Equally, there is no *generic* skill of understanding metaphors; in any lesson, we can only teach children about *specific* metaphors. A dot here, a dot there, and over time the expertise of reading emerges for each child like a pointillist landscape. This may sound awfully gradual, but teaching reading is an incremental process in which every lesson is a tiny contribution to something vast. We should face the reality of it, in all of its painstaking magnificence and adapt our instruction accordingly.

Second, pointillism is founded on an intimate relationship between art and science. Arguably the greatest of the pointillist painters was Georges Seurat. Like all artists, his work was based on the instincts gained from personal experience. However, to create his masterpieces he interpreted the theories of colour produced by the scientists of his time. On this basis, Seurat placed constituent colours beside one another and relied on the eye's natural inclination to blend the two. The resulting paintings are a glorious testament to what can be achieved when the refined instincts of the experienced artist are informed by the power of science. In exactly this way – and as this book has argued – understanding the science of reading can, and should, transform the art of classroom teaching.

GLOSSARY

accuracy   one of three elements of reading fluency; it relates to a child's ability to correctly match the spelling of a word to the sounds it represents.

advanced code   the sound–spelling correspondences taught after the initial/basic code (comprising the most common spellings for each phoneme) has been taught.

alphabetic principle   the understanding that there are relationships between written letters and sounds.

analogy phonics   instruction in sound–spelling correspondences and phonemic awareness skills that relies on children combining parts of words they have already memorised to decode unfamiliar words; this form of phonics requires children to memorise a cache of sight words that can be used to decode other words.

analytic phonics   instruction in sound–spelling correspondences and phonemic awareness skills that relies on children analysing whole words to find patterns of sound between them; this form of phonics requires children to memorise a cache of sight words that can be used to decode other words.

anaphor   a word or phrase that refers back to an earlier word or phrase and relies upon the earlier word or phrase for its meaning.

automaticity   one of three elements of reading fluency; it relates to a child's ability to decode a word rapidly and without a great deal of conscious thought; it is more likely to be achieved once many of the words being read have been orthographically mapped.

background knowledge   a reader's knowledge of the world that relates to the text being read.

blending   the combining of individual sounds in a word to recreate the word as it would be spoken aloud.

close reading   a form of reading lesson that involves thoroughly analysing a text, often reading it repeatedly and looking at different aspects with each read.

comprehension monitoring the process of becoming aware of one's own level of understanding while reading and reacting to ensure that this understanding matches the goals set before reading.

comprehension strategies a blanket term for metacognitive aspects of reading that can be taught to ensure that the reader is taking responsibility for their own understanding of a text (e.g. self-questioning including summarising and visualising).

concept of word a reader's ability to match written words to spoken words while reading.

connective a word or phrase that is used to join words, phrases or sentences.

content area reading reading that develops knowledge of aspects of the broader school curriculum.

cueing systems strategies that children use to decode words that do not rely on their developing knowledge of sound–spelling correspondences, such as looking at pictures and using contextual clues; such strategies are associated with weaker readers and should be avoided as children first learn to read.

decodable book a book in which the vast majority of the sound–spelling correspondences are ones that a child has already been taught; given that all books are decodable (depending on the code knowledge of the reader), these are more accurately described as phonically controlled books.

decode to work out the word that is represented in writing; children need to learn to do this through the application of learned sound–spelling correspondences and phonemic awareness skills.

disciplinary knowledge the knowledge of how meaning in a discipline is gained, how it is scrutinised and how it is revised.

disciplinary reading reading that involves the development of the reader's disciplinary knowledge of a subject.

dyslexia a learning difficulty that affects the ease with which a person learns to read words; it is widely considered to have genetic, neurobiological causes.

elaborative inference an inference in which the reader speculates as to possibilities using information in a text.

encode to represent accurately the sounds of a word in writing.

extended reading a form of reading lesson involving discussion in which the majority of the lesson is spent reading text.

fluency the ability to read with accuracy, automaticity and prosody; put simply, reading with fluency involves correct decoding at an appropriate speed that allows for reading to sound like natural speech.

fluency practice a form of reading lesson involving repeated oral reading of a relatively short text and conscious attempts to read with greater fluency each time.

global coherence inference a gap-filling inference which relies on general knowledge or wider vocabulary to fill a gap that has been left by the writer; they might support an understanding of the setting, character motivations, themes or purpose of a text.

grapheme a written representation of a single phoneme in text.

inference the use of present information alongside reasoning to work out something that is not otherwise clearly stated.

initial/basic code the sound–spelling correspondences taught first in a phonics programme, comprising the most common spellings for each phoneme.

linguistic phonics instruction in sound–spelling correspondences and phonemic awareness skills that emphasises the sound-to-print orientation of writing; specifically, this involves teaching that the sounds are the basis of the written code both explicitly and implicitly.

local cohesion inference a text-connecting inference that directly connects elements within a text, often using single words or phrases such as anaphors or connectives.

metacognition being conscious about one's thinking; it can involve planning, monitoring and assessing one's understanding.

morpheme a meaningful element of language made up of a word or a part of a word that cannot be divided into smaller meaningful parts.

morphology the study of the internal structure of words, including the parts from which they are composed.

necessary inference an inference that is required for the reader to make sense of part of a text.

orthographic depth the extent to which there is a simple, one-to-one correspondence between sounds and spellings in a language; languages with a deep (or opaque) orthography, such as English, have multiple spellings that can represent a given sound and multiple sounds that can be represented by a given spelling.

orthographic mapping a process through which spellings of words become 'glued' to the pronunciations already stored in a reader's memory via repeated decoding; it leads to words being read without *conscious* decoding using learned sound–spelling correspondences.

orthography the conventional spelling system of a language.

phoneme the smallest distinguishable unit of sound in speech; this sound unit is the basis of written English.

phoneme deletion an activity that supports children's development of phonemic awareness in which a phoneme is removed from a word and the new word that is created is identified.

phoneme substitution an activity that supports children's development of phonemic awareness in which a phoneme is swapped for another and the new word that is created is identified.

phonemic awareness the extent to which someone is able to hear and manipulate phonemes in spoken language; it is one aspect of phonological awareness.

phonological awareness the extent to which someone is able to hear and manipulate the sounds in a spoken language, such as phonemes, syllables and whole words.

prefix a letter or group of letters placed at the start of a word that changes the word's meaning (e.g. historic → *pre*historic).

prosody the ability to read in a way that mirrors the sounds of natural spoken language; this includes intonation (the rise and fall in tone), stress (the prominence given to particular syllables, words or phrases) and rhythm.

root word a word that carries the most meaningful aspects of a word family; Latin and Greek root words often are not words when written on their own, but underpin the meaning of many words in English.

segmenting the separation and identification of sounds within a spoken word into individual phonemes.

shared reading a form of reading lesson in which a text is read aloud to children with brief discussion of vocabulary and key points; the central aim of such a session is enjoyment of a shared text and the development of listening comprehension.

sight word a word that is recognised without *conscious* decoding using learned sound–spelling correspondences; words become sight words through repeated decoding in a process called orthographic mapping.

simple view of reading   a view of reading that sees reading comprehension as consisting of two interacting components decoding and language comprehension; it is represented in the following equation:

   Decoding (D) × Language Comprehension (LC) = Reading Comprehension (RC)

situation model   a mentally constructed view of the contents of a text in which meaning is created and updated through a process of personalisation, prioritisation and integration.

sound–spelling correspondence   a systematic relationship between a sound and a spelling in a language.

standard of coherence   the level set by a reader relating to the expectation that a given text will make sense; expert readers tend to match their expected standard of coherence to their purpose for reading.

substantive knowledge   the knowledge produced by an academic subject and thus taught as established fact.

suffix   a letter or group of letters placed at the end of a word that changes the word's meaning (e.g. quick → quick*ly*).

synthetic phonics   instruction in sound–spelling correspondences and phonemic awareness skills that explicitly shows learners the relationships between sounds and spellings from the beginning.

tier one word   a word that commonly appears in spoken language.

tier three word   a word that does not commonly appear in spoken language and is specific to given academic subjects; these words are often taught in the relevant academic subjects.

tier two word   a word that does not commonly appear in spoken language, is not specific to given academic subject and thus has broader utility.

vocabulary breadth   the number of words recognised by a person.

vocabulary depth   the extent to which the words recognised by a person are understood in a variety of contexts with a variety of meanings.

APPENDIX A

THE '345 LIST' OF TIER TWO VOCABULARY FOR PRIMARY SCHOOLS

abandon
abstract
absolutely
access
accompany
accurate
achieve
acquire
adaptation
advantage
affect
aid
alter
alternative
analysis
announce
annual
anticipate
appearance
appreciation
approach
appropriate
area

assessment
association
assume
assumption
atmosphere
attached
attained
attitudes
attract
audience
authority
automatic
available
aware
basic
benefit
bond
brief
budget
capable
category
cease
channel

circumstances
civil
clarity
code
collapse
combine
comment
commit
common
communication
community
compare
complex
component
conceived
concept
conclusion
condition
confirmed
confined
conflict
conscious
consequences

consider	draft	file
consistent	duration	final
constant	dynamic	flexibility
construction	economy	focus
contact	efficient	format
context	eliminate	foundation
contract	emerged	framework
contrast	emphasis	frequent
contribution	enable	furthermore
control	encounter	generated
controversial	energy	global
converted	enhanced	goals
convinced	ensure	government
co-operation	entire	guarantee
core	environment	hierarchy
couple	equipment	highlighted
create	error	identical
crucial	establish	identified
cultural	estimate	ignored
cycle	ethical	image
data	evaluation	impact
debate	eventually	imposed
decline	evidence	incident
definite	evolution	indicate
definition	examine	individual
demonstrate	example	inferred
deny	exceed	influence
design	exchange	initial
despite	excluded	innovation
detect	exhibit	input
develop	exist	insert
device	expansion	insight
dimension	experience	instruction
discrimination	expert	intelligence
display	exploitation	intensity
distorted	external	intention
distribute	extract	interaction
diversity	factor	internal
document	familiar	international
dominant	features	investigate

involved

isolated

issues

justification

label

layer

limit

link

literature

location

logic

maintain

major

market

maximum

media

medium

mental

method

migration

military

minimum

monitoring

motivation

national

necessary

negotiation

neutral

nevertheless

nonetheless

object

objective

obtained

obvious

occur

odd

option

organise

outcomes

overall

overcome

overseas

period

persistent

perspective

phase

phenomenon

philosophy

physical

political

popular

positive

possession

potential

precise

predicted

previous

principle

prior

priority

procedure

process

prohibited

propose

prospect

public

published

pursue

quotation

random

reaction

recognise

recovery

refine

region

rejected

related

release

reluctant

removed

represent

required

research

reserve

resources

response

restore

retained

revealed

reverse

revision

revolution

rigid

role

route

schedule

scheme

section

security

select

sensitive

separate

sequence

series

severe

shift

signal

significant

similar

site

society

solely

source

specific

stability

standard

strategies

structure

style

subsequent

substitution

sufficient

suitable

summary	tension	typical
supply	text	underlying
support	theme	unique
survive	theory	united
sustainable	traditional	variation
symbol	transfer	via
system	transform	visible
target	transition	visual
technique	transport	volume
technology	trend	voluntary
temporary	trigger	whereas

APPENDIX B

LATIN AND GREEK ROOT WORDS FOR PRIMARY SCHOOLS

acro – top, height (e.g. acrobat, acronym, acropolis)

act/ag – do (e.g. action, agent, agitate)

acu – sharp (e.g. accurate, acupuncture, acute)

aero – air (e.g. aerial, aeronaut, aerospace)

ali/alter – other (e.g. alias, alien, alter)

ambi – both (e.g. ambidextrous, ambiguous, ambivalent)

anni/annu – year (e.g. anniversary, annual, annually)

anti – opposite (e.g. antibiotic, anticlockwise, antisocial)

aqu – water (e.g. aquarium, aquatic, aqueduct)

astro – star (e.g. asterisk, astronaut, astronomer)

aud – hear (e.g. audible, audience, audio)

auto – self (e.g. autograph, automatic, automobile)

bi – two, twice (e.g. bicycle, binoculars, biped)

bibl – book (e.g. bible, bibliography, bibliophile)

bio – life (e.g. biography, biology, biosphere)

capt/cept – hold, take (e.g. captivate, intercept, receipt)

carn – flesh (e.g. carnal, carnivore, incarnate)

cent – hundred (e.g. centimetre, centipede, century)

cert – sure (e.g. ascertain, certain, certificate)

chrono – time (e.g. chronic, chronological, chronometer)

cide/cise – cut, kill (e.g. excise, homicide, incisor)

claim/clam – speak out (e.g. clamour, exclamation, proclamation)

clar – clear (e.g. clarify, clarity, declare)

cline – lean (e.g. inclination, incline, recline)

clud/clus – close (e.g. conclude, exclude, seclude)

co – together (e.g. co-author, coexist, cooperate)

cogn – know (e.g. cognition, incognito, recognise)

com – together (e.g. communicate, community, composition)

con – with (e.g. concur, contemporary, convention)

contra – against (e.g. contradict, contrary, controversy)

corp – body (e.g. corporal, corporation, corpse)

cosm – universe (e.g. cosmic, cosmos, microcosm)

cred – belief (e.g. credit, credulous, incredible)

cycl – circle (e.g. bicycle, cyclone, tricycle)

de – reduce (e.g. debug, decelerate, dethrone)

dec – ten (e.g. decade, decathlon, December)

demo – people (e.g. democracy, demonstrate, epidemic)

dent – teeth (e.g. dentist, dentures, trident)

dia – through/across (e.g. diagonal, diagram, diameter)

dict – speak (e.g. contradict, dictionary, prediction)

dis – away (e.g. disagree, disappear, disqualify)

domin – master (e.g. dominate, domineering, dominion)

don – give (e.g. donate, donor, pardon)

du – two (e.g. duet, duo, duplicate)

dur – last (e.g. durable, duration, endure)

dyn – power (e.g. dynamic, dynamite, dynamo)

equ – equal (e.g. equal, equanimity, equidistant)

ex – out (e.g. exclaim, exclude, exhale)

extr – beyond (e.g. extraordinary, extra-terrestrial, extrovert)

fer – carry (e.g. ferry, refer, transfer)

fid – faith (e.g. confide, confident, fidelity)

flect/flex – bend (e.g. flexible, inflect, reflect)

fore – in front of (e.g. forebode, forecast, forefather)

form – shape (e.g. deform, reform, uniform)

fug – run away (e.g. fugitive, refuge, refugee)

gen – birth (e.g. generate, genesis, genetic)

geo – earth (e.g. geography, geology, geometry)

gon – angle (e.g. diagonal, hexagon, polygon)

graph – writing (e.g. autograph, biography, graphics)

herb – plant (e.g. herbal, herbicide, herbivore)

hydro – water (e.g. dehydrate, hydrate, hydrogen)

il/im/in/ir – not, without (e.g. illegal, impossible, inappropriate, irrational)

inter – between (e.g. intercept, international, intersection)

ject – throw (e.g. eject, project, reject)

jud – law (e.g. judge, judiciary, prejudice)

kilo – thousand (e.g. kilogram, kilometre, kilowatt)

lab – work (e.g. collaborate, laboratory, labour)

liber – free (e.g. liberal, liberate, liberty)

loc – place (e.g. dislocate, location, relocate)

log – word (e.g. analogy, catalogue, dialogue)

lun – moon (e.g. lunacy, lunar, lunatic)

magna – great, large (e.g. magnate, magnificent, magnify)

mal – bad (e.g. malfunction, malicious, malnourished)

mand – order (e.g. command, demand, mandatory)

mar – sea (e.g. marine, maritime, submarine)

mater – mother (e.g. maternal, maternity, matriarch)

max – greatest (e.g. maximal, maximise, maximum)

medi – middle (e.g. medieval, mediocre, medium)

memor – remember (e.g. commemorate, memorial, memory)

micro – very small (e.g. microbe, microchip, microscope)

mid – middle (e.g. mid-air, midday, midriff)

milli – thousandth (e.g. millilitre, millimetre, millipede)

mini – small (e.g. miniature, minimum, minuscule)

mis – wrong (e.g. misbehave, misprint, mistake)

mono – one (e.g. monochrome, monologue, monotheism)

mort – death (e.g. immortal, mortal, mortician)

nat – birth (e.g. innate, nativity, natural)

neg – no (e.g. negate, negative, renege)

nom – name (e.g. denominator, nominate, nomination)

non – not (e.g. nondescript, nonfiction, nonsense)

nov – new (e.g. innovate, novelty, novice)

numer – number (e.g. enumerate, numerator, numerous)

oct – eight (e.g. octagon, octogenarian, octopus)

omni – all (e.g. omnipotent, omniscient, omnivore)

para – beside (e.g. parachute, parallel, parasite)

path – feeling (e.g. antipathy, empathy, sympathy)

ped – foot (e.g. pedal, pedestal, pedestrian)

pel – force (e.g. compel, expel, repel)

pent – five (e.g. pentagon, pentagram, pentathlon)

per – throughout (e.g. perennial, permanent, persist)

phon – sound (e.g. cacophony, microphone, telephone)

photo – light (e.g. photogenic, photograph, photon)

poli – city (e.g. metropolis, police, politics)

poly – many (e.g. polygon, polymer, polytheism)

pop – people (e.g. populace, popular, population)

port – carry (e.g. export, import, portable)

pos – put (e.g. deposit, dispose, expose)

post – after (e.g. posthumous, postpone, postscript)

pre – before (e.g. preclude, prediction, prepare)

pro – before (e.g. prognosis, prologue, prophet)

pul – urge (e.g. compulsion, expulsion, impulsive)

quad – four (e.g. quad bike, quadrilateral, quadruped)

quart – fourth (e.g. quart, quarter, quartet)

re – again (e.g. reaction, rebound, rewind)

reg – rule (e.g. regal, regent, regulate)

rupt – break (e.g. bankrupt, corrupt, interrupt)

scend – climb (e.g. ascend, crescendo, descend)

sci – know (e.g. conscience, conscious, science)

scope – see (e.g. microscope, periscope, telescope)

scribe/scrip – write (e.g. describe, inscribe, script)

sect – cut (e.g. bisect, dissect, section)

sed/sid – sit (e.g. preside, sedentary, sediment)

serv – keep (e.g. conserve, preserve, reserve)

sol – alone (e.g. desolate, solitary, solo)

spec – look (e.g. inspect, spectacle, spectator)

sta – stand (e.g. stable, stagnant, stationary)

struct – build (e.g. construct, destruction, structure)

sub – below (e.g. submarine, submerge, substandard)

super – higher (e.g. superior, supernatural, supersonic)

tact – touch (e.g. contact, intact, tactile)

tele – far (e.g. telephone, telescope, television)

terr – land (e.g. extra-terrestrial, terrain, territory)

tract – pull (e.g. contract, retract, tractor)

trans – across (e.g. transfer, transparent, transport)

tri – three (e.g. triangle, tricycle, tripod)

un – not (e.g. undone, unfair, unfriendly)

uni – one (e.g. unicycle, unison, universe)

vac – empty (e.g. evacuate, vacant, vacuum)

ver – truth (e.g. aver, verdict, verify)

verb – word (e.g. adverb, proverb, verbal)

vers/vert – turn (e.g. extrovert, introvert, reverse)

vid – see (e.g. evidence, provide, video)

APPENDIX C
EXAMPLE TIMETABLES FOR EXPLICIT VOCABULARY INSTRUCTION

Year 3				
Week	Root word (Monday)	Tier two vocabulary (Tuesday)	Retrieval (Wednesday)	Retrieval (Thursday)	Quiz of week's content (Friday)
1	*acro* – top, height (e.g. acrobat, acronym, acropolis)	achieve affect			
2	*act/ag* – do (e.g. action, agent, agitate)	aid alter			
3	*acu* – sharp (e.g. accurate, acupuncture, acute)	appearance area			
4	*aero* – air (e.g. aerial, aeronaut, aerospace)	attached audience			
5	*ali/alter* – other (e.g. alias, alien, alter)	basic capable	*acro* – top, height (e.g. acrobat, acronym, acropolis)	achieve affect	
6	*ambi* – both (e.g. ambidextrous, ambiguous, ambivalent)	collapse combine	*act/ag* – do (e.g. action, agenda, agent, agitate)	aid alter	
7	*anni/annu* – year (e.g. anniversary, annual, annually)	comment common	*acu* – sharp (e.g. acupuncture, accurate, acute)	appearance area	

(Continued)

Year 3				
Week	**Root word** **(Monday)**	**Tier two vocabulary** **(Tuesday)**	**Retrieval** **(Wednesday)**	**Retrieval** **(Thursday)**	**Quiz of week's content** **(Friday)**
8	*anti* – opposite (e.g. antibiotic, anticlockwise, antisocial)	compare conclusion	*aero* – air (e.g. aerial, aerospace)	attached audience	
9	*aqu* – water (e.g. aquarium, aquatic, aqueduct)	consequences constant	*ali/alter* – other (e.g. alias, alien, alter, altruism)	basic capable	
10	*astro* – star (e.g. asterisk, astronaut, astronomer)	contact control	*ambi* – both (e.g. ambidextrous, ambiguous, ambivalent)	collapse combine	
11	*aud* – hear (e.g. audible, audience, audio)	cooperation core	*anni/annu* – year (e.g. anniversary, annual, annually)	comment common	
12	*auto* – self (e.g. autograph, automatic, automobile)	create cycle	*anti* – opposite (e.g. antibiotic, anticlockwise, antisocial)	compare conclusion	
13	*bi* – two, twice (e.g. bicycle, binoculars, biped)	diversity draft	*aqu* – water (e.g. aquarium, aquatic, aqueduct)	consequences constant	
14	*bibl* – book (e.g. bible, bibliography, bibliophile)	enable energy	*astro* – star (e.g. asterisk, astronaut, astronomer)	contact control	
15	*bio* – life (e.g. biography, biology, biosphere)	entire equipment	*aud* – hear (e.g. audible, audience, audio)	cooperation core	
16	*capt/cept* – hold, take (e.g. captivate, intercept, receipt)	error examine	*auto* – self (e.g. autograph, automatic, automobile)	create cycle	
17	*carn* – flesh (e.g. carnal, carnivore, incarnate)	example exchange	*bi* – two, twice (e.g. bicycle, binoculars, biped)	diversity draft	
18	*cent* – hundred (e.g. centimetre, centipede, century)	exhibit expert	*bibl* – book (e.g. bible, bibliography, bibliophile)	enable energy	

Year 3				
Week	**Root word** **(Monday)**	**Tier two vocabulary** **(Tuesday)**	**Retrieval** **(Wednesday)**	**Retrieval** **(Thursday)**	**Quiz of week's content** **(Friday)**
19	*cert* – sure (e.g. ascertain, certain, certificate)	external extract	*bio* – life (e.g. biography, biology, biosphere)	entire equipment	
20	*chrono* – time (e.g. chronic, chronological, chronometer)	final frequent	*capt/cept* – hold, take (e.g. captivate, intercept, receipt)	error examine	
21	*cide/cise* – cut, kill (e.g. excise, homicide, incisor)	goals identical	*carn* – flesh (e.g. carnal, carnivore, incarnate)	example exchange	
22	*circ* – ring (e.g. circle, circuit, circus)	ignored image	*cent* – hundred (e.g. centipede, centimetre, century)	exhibit expert	
23	*claim/clam* – speak out (e.g. clamour, exclamation, proclamation)	individual insert	*cert* – sure (e.g. ascertain, certain, certificate)	external extract	
24	*clar* – clear (e.g. clarify, clarity, declare)	intelligence label	*chrono* – time (e.g. chronic, chronological, chronometer)	final frequent	
25	*cline* – lean (e.g. inclination, incline, recline)	layer location	*cide/cise* – cut, kill (e.g. excise, homicide, incisor)	goals identical	
26	*clud/clus* – close (e.g. conclude, exclude, seclude)	method object	*circ* – ring (e.g. circle, circuit, circus)	ignored image	
27	*co* – together (e.g. co-author, coexist, cooperate)	odd popular	*claim/clam* – speak out (e.g. clamour, exclamation, proclamation)	individual insert	
28	*cogn* – know (e.g. cognition, incognito, recognise)	positive prohibited	*clar* – clear (e.g. clarify, clarity, declare)	intelligence label	
29	*com* – together (e.g. communicate, community, composition)	pursue recognise	*cline* – lean (e.g. inclination, incline, recline)	layer location	

(Continued)

Year 3					
Week	**Root word** **(Monday)**	**Tier two vocabulary** **(Tuesday)**	**Retrieval** **(Wednesday)**	**Retrieval** **(Thursday)**	**Quiz of week's content** **(Friday)**
30	*con* – with (e.g. concur, contemporary, convention)	release restore	*clud/clus* – close (e.g. conclude, exclude, seclude)	method object	
31	*contra* – against (e.g. contradict, contrary, controversy)	reverse rigid	*co* – together (e.g. co-author, coexist, cooperate)	odd popular	
32	*corp* – body (e.g. corporal, corporation, corpse)	shift survive	*cogn* – know (e.g. cognition, recognise, incognito)	positive prohibited	
33	*cosm* – universe (e.g. cosmic, cosmos, microcosm)	symbol target	*com* – together (e.g. communicate, community, composition)	pursue recognise	
34	*cred* – belief (e.g. credit, credulous, incredible)	unique visible	*con* – with (e.g. concur, contemporary, convention)	release restore	

Year 4					
Week	**Root word** **(Monday)**	**Tier two vocabulary** **(Tuesday)**	**Retrieval** **(Wednesday)**	**Retrieval** **(Thursday)**	**Quiz of week's content** **(Friday)**
1	*cycl* – circle (e.g. bicycle, cyclone, tricycle)	abandon accompany	*contra* – against (e.g. contradict, contrary, controversy)	reverse rigid	
2	*de* – reduce (e.g. debug, decelerate, dethrone)	accurate acquire	*corp* – body (e.g. corporal, corporation, corpse)	shift survive	
3	*dec* – ten (e.g. decade, decathlon, December)	advantage announce	*cosm* – universe (e.g. cosmic, cosmos, microcosm)	symbol target	
4	*demo* – people (e.g. democracy, demonstrate, epidemic)	annual approach	*cred* – belief (e.g. credit, credulous, incredible)	unique visible	
5	*dent* – teeth (e.g. dentist, dentures, trident)	appropriate attract	*cycl* – circle (e.g. bicycle, cyclone, tricycle)	abandon accompany	
6	*dia* – through/across (e.g. diagonal, diagram, diameter)	aware brief	*de* – reduce (e.g. debug, decelerate, dethrone)	accurate acquire	

Year 4				
Week	Root word (Monday)	Tier two vocabulary (Tuesday)	Retrieval (Wednesday)	Retrieval (Thursday)	Quiz of week's content (Friday)
7	*dict* – speak (e.g. contradict, dictionary, prediction)	cease component	*dec* – ten (e.g. decade, decathlon, December)	advantage announce	
8	*dis* – away (e.g. disagree, disappear, disqualify)	consider converted	*demo* – people (e.g. democracy, demonstrate, epidemic)	annual approach	
9	*domin* – master (e.g. dominate, domineering, dominion)	convinced couple	*dent* – teeth (e.g. dentist, dentures, trident)	appropriate attract	
10	*don* – give (e.g. donate, donor, pardon)	crucial debate	*dia* – through/across (e.g. diagonal, diagram, diameter)	aware brief	
11	*du* – two (e.g. duet, duo, duplicate)	definite deny	*dict* – speak (e.g. contradict, dictionary, prediction)	cease component	
12	*dur* – last (e.g. durable, duration, endure)	detect display	*dis* – away (e.g. disagree, disappear, disqualify)	consider converted	
13	*equ* – equal (e.g. equal, equanimity, equidistant)	document efficient	*domin* – master (e.g. dominate, domineering, dominion)	convinced couple	
14	*ex* – out (e.g. exclude, exclaim, exhale)	ensure estimate	*don* – give (e.g. donate, donor, pardon)	crucial debate	
15	*extr* – beyond (e.g. extraordinary, extra-terrestrial, extrovert)	exceed flexibility	*du* – two (e.g. duet, duo, duplicate)	definite deny	
16	*fer* – carry (e.g. ferry, refer, transfer)	initial instruction	*dur* – last (e.g. durable, duration, endure)	detect display	
17	*fid* – faith (e.g. confide, confident, fidelity)	internal link	*equ* – equal (e.g. equal, equanimity, equidistant)	document efficient	
18	*flect/flex* – bend (e.g. flexible, inflect, reflect)	major maximum	*ex* – out (e.g. exclaim, exclude, exhale)	ensure estimate	
19	*fore* – in front of (e.g. forebode, forecast, forefather)	minimum obtained	*extr* – beyond (e.g. extraordinary, extra-terrestrial, extrovert)	exceed flexibility	
20	*form* – shape (e.g. deform, reform, uniform)	obvious possession	*fer* – carry (e.g. ferry, refer, transfer)	initial instruction	

(Continued)

Year 4				
Week	**Root word** **(Monday)**	**Tier two vocabulary** **(Tuesday)**	**Retrieval** **(Wednesday)**	**Retrieval** **(Thursday)**	**Quiz of week's content** **(Friday)**
21	*fug* – run away (e.g. fugitive, refuge, refugee)	predicted previous	*fid* – faith (e.g. confide, confident, fidelity)	internal link	
22	*gen* – birth (e.g. generate, genesis, genetic)	prior public	*flect/flex* – bend (e.g. flexible, inflect, reflect)	major maximum	
23	*geo* – earth (e.g. geography, geology, geometry)	recovery rejected	*fore* – in front of (e.g. forecast, forebode, forefather)	minimum obtained	
24	*gon* – angle (e.g. diagonal, hexagon, polygon)	research select	*form* – shape (e.g. deform, reform, uniform)	obvious possession	
25	*graph* – writing (e.g. autograph, biography, graphics)	sequence stability	*fug* – run away (e.g. fugitive, refuge, refugee)	predicted previous	
26	*herb* – plant (e.g. herbal, herbicide, herbivore)	structure suitable	*gen* – birth (e.g. generate, genesis, genetic)	prior public	
27	*hexa* – six (e.g. hexagon, hexameter, hexapod)	supply support	*geo* – earth (e.g. geography, geology, geometry)	recovery rejected	
28	*hydro* – water (e.g. dehydrate, hydrate, hydrogen)	technology text	*gon* – angle (e.g. diagonal, hexagon, polygon)	research select	
29	*il/im/in/ir* – not, without (e.g. illegal, impossible, inappropriate, irrational)	typical united	*graph* – writing (e.g. autograph, biography, graphics)	sequence stability	
30	*inter* – between (e.g. intercept, international, intersection)	evidence option	*herb* – plant (e.g. herbal, herbicide, herbivore)	structure suitable	
31	*ject* – throw (e.g. eject, project, reject)	excluded market	*hexa* – six (e.g. hexagon, hexameter, hexapod)	supply support	
32	*jud* – law (e.g. judge, judiciary, prejudice)	removed site	*hydro* – water (e.g. dehydrate, hydrate, hydrogen)	technology text	

Year 4					
Week	Root word (Monday)	Tier two vocabulary (Tuesday)	Retrieval (Wednesday)	Retrieval (Thursday)	Quiz of week's content (Friday)
33	*kilo* – thousand (e.g. kilogram, kilometre, kilowatt)	similar temporary	*il/im/in/ir* – not, without (e.g. illegal, impossible, inappropriate, irrational)	typical united	
34	*lab* – work (e.g. collaborate, laboratory, labour)	transform volume	*inter* – between (e.g. intercept, international, intersection)	evidence option	

Year 5					
Week	Root word (Monday)	Tier two vocabulary (Tuesday)	Retrieval (Wednesday)	Retrieval (Thursday)	Quiz of week's content (Friday)
1	*liber* – free (e.g. liberal, liberate, liberty)	abstract ethical phase	*ject* – throw (e.g. eject, project, reject)	excluded market	
2	*loc* – place (e.g. dislocate, location, relocate)	absolutely evaluation phenomenon	*jud* – law (e.g. judge, judiciary, prejudice)	removed site	
3	*log* – word (e.g. analogy, catalogue, dialogue)	access eventually philosophy	*kilo* – thousand (e.g. kilogram, kilometre, kilowatt)	similar temporary	
4	*lun* – moon (e.g. lunacy, lunar, lunatic)	adaptation evolution physical	*lab* – work (e.g. collaborate, laboratory, labour)	transform volume	
5	*magna* – great, large (e.g. magnate, magnificent, magnify)	alternative exist political	*liber* – free (e.g. liberal, liberate, liberty)	abstract ethical phase	
6	*mal* – bad (e.g. malfunction, malicious, malnourished)	analysis expansion potential	*loc* – place (e.g. dislocate, location, relocate)	absolutely evaluation phenomenon	
7	*mand* – order (e.g. command, demand, mandatory)	anticipate experience precise	*log* – word (e.g. analogy, catalogue, dialogue)	access eventually philosophy	

(Continued)

Year 5				
Week	Root word (Monday)	Tier two vocabulary (Tuesday)	Retrieval (Wednesday)	Retrieval (Thursday)	Quiz of week's content (Friday)
8	*mar* – sea (e.g. marine, maritime, submarine)	appreciation exploitation principle	*lun* – moon (e.g. lunacy, lunar, lunatic)	adaptation evolution physical	
9	*mater* – mother (e.g. maternal, maternity, matriarch)	assessment factor priority	*magna* – great, large (e.g. magnate, magnificent, magnify)	alternative exist political	
10	*max* – greatest (e.g. maximal, maximise, maximum)	association familiar procedure	*mal* – bad (e.g. malfunction, malicious, malnourished)	analysis expansion potential	
11	*medi* – middle (e.g. medieval, mediocre, medium)	assume features process	*mand* – order (e.g. command, demand, mandatory)	anticipate experience precise	
12	*memor* – remember (e.g. commemorate, memorial, memory)	atmosphere file propose	*mar* – sea (e.g. marine, maritime, submarine)	appreciation exploitation principle	
13	*micro* – very small (e.g. microbe, microchip, microscope)	attained focus prospect	*mater* – mother (e.g. maternal, maternity, matriarch)	assessment factor priority	
14	*mid* – middle (e.g. mid-air, midday, midriff)	attitudes format published	*max* – greatest (e.g. maximal, maximise, maximum)	association familiar procedure	
15	*milli* – thousandth (e.g. millilitre, millimetre, millipede)	authority foundation random	*medi* – middle (e.g. medieval, mediocre, medium)	assume features process	
16	*mini* – small (e.g. miniature, minimum, minuscule)	automatic framework reaction	*memor* – remember (e.g. commemorate, memorial, memory)	atmosphere file propose	
17	*mis* – wrong (e.g. misbehave, misprint, mistake)	available generated refine	*micro* – very small (e.g. microbe, microchip, microscope)	attained focus prospect	

Year 5				
Week	Root word (Monday)	Tier two vocabulary (Tuesday)	Retrieval (Wednesday)	Retrieval (Thursday)	Quiz of week's content (Friday)
18	*mono* – one (e.g. monochrome, monologue, monotheism)	benefit global region	*mid* – middle (e.g. mid-air, midday, midriff)	attitudes format published	
19	*mort* – death (e.g. immortal, mortal, mortician)	bond government related	*milli* – thousandth (e.g. millilitre, millimetre, millipede)	authority foundation random	
20	*nat* – birth (e.g. innate, nativity, natural)	budget guarantee reluctant	*mini* – small (e.g. miniature, minimum, minuscule)	automatic framework reaction	
21	*neg* – no (e.g. negate, negative, renege)	category hierarchy represent	*mis* – wrong (e.g. misbehave, misprint, mistake)	available generated refine	
22	*nom* – name (e.g. denominator, nominate, nomination)	channel highlighted required	*mono* – one (e.g. monochrome, monologue, monotheism)	benefit global region	
23	*non* – not (e.g. nondescript, nonfiction, nonsense)	circumstances identified reserve	*mort* – death (e.g. immortal, mortal, mortician)	bond government related	
24	*nov* – new (e.g. innovate, novelty, novice)	civil impact resources	*nat* – birth (e.g. innate, nativity, natural)	budget guarantee reluctant	
25	*numer* – number (e.g. enumerate, numerator, numerous)	clarity imposed response	*neg* – no (e.g. negate, negative, renege)	category hierarchy represent	
26	*oct* – eight (e.g. octagon, octogenarian, octopus)	code incident retained	*nom* – name (e.g. denominator, nominate, nomination)	channel highlighted required	
27	*omni* – all (e.g. omnipotent, omniscient, omnivore)	commit indicate revealed	*non* – not (e.g. nondescript, nonfiction, nonsense)	circumstances identified reserve	
28	*para* – beside (e.g. parachute, parallel, parasite)	communication inferred revision	*nov* – new (e.g. innovate, novelty, novice)	civil impact resources	

(Continued)

Year 5				
Week	**Root word** (Monday)	**Tier two vocabulary** (Tuesday)	**Retrieval** (Wednesday)	**Retrieval** (Thursday)	**Quiz of week's content** (Friday)
29	*path* – feeling (e.g. antipathy, empathy, sympathy)	community influence revolution	*numer* – number (e.g. enumerate, numerator, numerous)	clarity imposed response	
30	*ped* – foot (e.g. pedal, pedestal, pedestrian)	complex innovation role	*oct* – eight (e.g. octagon, octogenarian, octopus)	code incident retained	
31	*pel* – force (e.g. compel, expel, repel)	conceived input route	*omni* – all (e.g. omnipotent, omniscient, omnivore)	commit indicate revealed	
32	*penta* – five (e.g. pentagon, pentagram, pentathlon)	concept insight schedule	*para* – beside (e.g. parachute, parallel, parasite)	communication inferred revision	
33	*per* – throughout (e.g. perennial, permanent, persist)	condition intensity scheme	*path* – feeling (e.g. antipathy, empathy, sympathy)	community influence revolution	
34	*phon* – sound (e.g. cacophony, microphone, telephone)	confirmed intention section	*ped* – foot (e.g. pedal, pedestal, pedestrian)	complex innovation role	

Year 6				
Week	**Root word** (Monday)	**Tier two vocabulary** (Tuesday)	**Retrieval** (Wednesday)	**Retrieval** (Thursday)	**Quiz of week's content** (Friday)
1	*photo* – light (e.g. photogenic, photograph, photon)	confined interaction security	*pel* – force (e.g. compel, expel, repel)	conceived input route	
2	*poli* – city (e.g. metropolis, police, politics)	conflict international sensitive	*penta* – five (e.g. pentagon, pentagram, pentathlon)	concept insight schedule	
3	*poly* – many (e.g. polygon, polymer, polytheism)	conscious investigate separate	*per* – throughout (e.g. perennial, permanent, persist)	condition intensity scheme	
4	*pop* – people (e.g. populace, popular, population)	consistent involved series	*phon* – sound (e.g. cacophony, microphone, telephone)	confirmed intention section	

Year 6					
Week	Root word (Monday)	Tier two vocabulary (Tuesday)	Retrieval (Wednesday)	Retrieval (Thursday)	Quiz of week's content (Friday)
5	*port* – carry (e.g. export, import, portable)	construction isolated severe	*photo* – light (e.g. photogenic, photograph, photon)	confined interaction security	
6	*pos* – put (e.g. expose, deposit, dispose)	context issues signal	*poli* – city (e.g. metropolis, police, politics)	conflict international sensitive	
7	*post* – after (e.g. posthumous, postpone, postscript)	contract justification significant	*poly* – many (e.g. polygon, polymer, polytheism)	conscious investigate separate	
8	*pre* – before (e.g. preclude, prediction, prepare)	contrast limit society	*pop* – people (e.g. populace, popular, population)	consistent involved series	
9	*pro* – before (e.g. prognosis, prologue, prophet)	contribution literature solely	*port* – carry (e.g. export, import, portable)	construction isolated severe	
10	*pul* – urge (e.g. compulsion, expulsion, impulsive)	control logic source	*pos* – put (e.g. deposit, dispose, expose)	context issues signal	
11	*quad* – four (e.g. quad bike, quadrilateral, quadruped)	controversial maintain specific	*post* – after (e.g. posthumous, postpone, postscript)	contract justification significant	
12	*quart* – fourth (e.g. quart, quarter, quartet)	cultural media standard	*pre* – before (e.g. preclude, prediction, prepare)	contrast limit society	
13	*re* – again (e.g. reaction, rebound, rewind)	data medium strategies	*pro* – before (e.g. prognosis, prologue, prophet)	contribution literature solely	
14	*reg* – rule (e.g. regal, regent, regulate)	decline mental style	*pul* – urge (e.g. compulsion, expulsion, impulsive)	control logic source	
15	*rupt* – break (e.g. bankrupt, corrupt, interrupt)	definition migration subsequent	*quad* – four (e.g. quad bike, quadrilateral, quadruped)	controversial maintain specific	
16	*scend* – climb (e.g. ascend, crescendo, descend)	demonstrate military substitution	*quart* – fourth (e.g. quart, quarter, quartet)	cultural media standard	

(Continued)

Year 6				
Week	**Root word** **(Monday)**	**Tier two vocabulary** **(Tuesday)**	**Retrieval** **(Wednesday)**	**Retrieval** **(Thursday)**	**Quiz of week's content (Friday)**
17	*sci* – know (e.g. conscience, conscious, science)	design monitoring sufficient	*re* – again (e.g. reaction, rebound, rewind)	data medium strategies	
18	*scope* – see (e.g. microscope, periscope, telescope)	despite motivation summary	*reg* – rule (e.g. regal, regent, regulate)	decline mental style	
19	*scribe/scrip* – write (e.g. describe, inscribe, script)	develop national sustainable	*rupt* – break (e.g. bankrupt, corrupt, interrupt)	definition migration subsequent	
20	*sect* – cut (e.g. bisect, dissect, section)	device necessary system	*scend* – climb (e.g. ascend, crescendo, descend)	demonstrate military substitution	
21	*sed/sid* – sit (e.g. preside, sedentary, sediment)	dimension negotiation technique	*sci* – know (e.g. conscience, conscious, science)	design monitoring sufficient	
22	*semi* – half (e.g. semicircle, semicolon, semi-final)	discrimination neutral tension	*scope* – see (e.g. microscope, periscope, telescope)	despite motivation summary	
23	*serv* – keep (e.g. conserve, preserve, reserve)	distorted nevertheless theme	*scribe/scrip* – write (e.g. describe, inscribe, script)	develop national sustainable	
24	*sol* – alone (e.g. desolate, solitary, solo)	distribute nonetheless theory	*sect* – cut (e.g. bisect, dissect, section)	device necessary system	
25	*spec* – look (e.g. inspect, spectacle, spectator)	dominant objective traditional	*sed/sid* – sit (e.g. preside, sedentary, sediment)	dimension negotiation technique	
26	*sta* – stand (e.g. stable, stagnant, stationary)	duration occur transfer	*semi* – half (e.g. semicircle, semicolon, semi-final)	discrimination neutral tension	
27	*struct* – build (e.g. construct, destruction, structure) *sub* – below (e.g. submarine, submerge, substandard)	economy organise transport	*serv* – keep (e.g. conserve, preserve, reserve)	distorted nevertheless theme	

Year 6				
Week	Root word (Monday)	Tier two vocabulary (Tuesday)	Retrieval (Wednesday)	Retrieval (Thursday)	Quiz of week's content (Friday)
28	*super* – higher (e.g. superior, supernatural, supersonic) *tact* – contact, touch (e.g. intact, tactile)	eliminate outcomes transition	*sol* – alone (e.g. desolate, solitary, solo)	distribute nonetheless theory	
29	*tele* – far (e.g. telephone, telescope, television) *terr* – land (e.g. extra-terrestrial, terrain, territory)	emerged overall trend	*spec* – look (e.g. inspect, spectacle, spectator)	dominant objective traditional	
30	*tract* – pull (e.g. contract, retract, tractor) *trans* – across (e.g. transfer, transparent, transport)	emphasis overcome trigger	*sta* – stand (e.g. stable, stagnant, stationary)	duration occur transfer	
31	*tri* – three (e.g. triangle, tricycle, tripod) *un* – not (e.g. undone, unfair, unfriendly)	encounter overseas underlying	*struct* – build (e.g. construct, destruction, structure) *sub* – below (e.g. submarine, submerge, substandard)	economy organise transport	
32	*uni* – one (e.g. unicycle, unison, universe) *vac* – empty (e.g. evacuate, vacant, vacuum)	enhanced period variation	*super* – higher (e.g. superior, supernatural, supersonic) *tact* – touch (e.g. contact, intact, tactile)	eliminate outcomes transition	
33	*ver* – truth (e.g. aver, verdict, verify) *verb* – word (e.g. adverb, proverb, verbal)	environment persistent visual	*tele* – far (e.g. telephone, telescope, television) *terr* – land (e.g. extra-terrestrial, terrain, territory)	emerged overall trend	
34	*vers/vert* – turn (e.g. extrovert, introvert, reverse) *vid* – see (e.g. evidence, provide, video)	establish perspective voluntary	*tract* – pull (e.g. contract, retract, tractor) *trans* – across (e.g. transfer, transparent, transport)	emphasis overcome trigger	

INDEX

Page numbers in *italics* refer to figures; page numbers in **bold** refer to tables.